Addictionary: A Primer of Recovery Terms and Concepts from Abstinence to Withdrawal, by Jan R. Wilson, C.E.D.C., C.A.P., and Judith A. Wilson, C.A.P.

Anatomy of a Food Addiction: The Brain Chemistry of Overeating, by Anne Katherine, M.A.

Behind the 8-Ball: A Guide for Families of Gamblers, by Linda Berman, M.S.W., and Mary-Ellen Siegel, M.S.W.

Believing in Myself: Daily Meditations for Healing and Building Self-Esteem, by Earnie Larsen and Carol Hegarty

Blues Ain't Nothing But a Good Soul Feeling Bad: Daily Steps to Spiritual Growth, by Sheldon Kopp with Bonnie B. Hesse

Codependents' Guide to the Twelve Steps, by Melody Beattie

Freedom from Food: The Secret Lives of Dieters and Compulsive Eaters, by Elizabeth Hampshire

From Love That Hurts to Love That's Real: A Recovery Workbook, by Sylvia Ogden Peterson

Growing Through the Pain: The Incest Survivor's Companion, by Catherine Bronson

Growing Up Gay in a Dysfunctional Family: A Guide for Gay Men Reclaiming Their Lives, by Rik Isensee

Help for Helpers: Daily Meditations for Those Who Care

Hooked on Exercise: How to Understand and Manage Exercise Addiction, by Rebecca Prussin, M.D., Philip Harvey, Ph.D., and Theresa Foy DiGeronimo

Meditations for Men Who Do Too Much, by Jonathon Lazear

Reclaiming Our Days: Meditations for Incest Survivors, by Helena See

Repressed Memories: A Journey to Recovery from Sexual Abuse, by Renee Fredrickson, Ph.D.

Soul Survivors: A New Beginning for Adults Abused as Children, by J. Patrick Gannon, Ph.D.

Understanding the Twelve Steps: An Interpretation and Guide for Recovering People, by Terence T. Gorski

Sex and Sobriety

Facing the Fear and Building a New Sexual Life

Jack Mumey

A FIRESIDE/PARKSIDE BOOK
Published by Simon&Schuster
New York London Toronto Sydney Tokyo Singapore

FIRESIDE/PARKSIDE
Simon & Schuster Building
Rockefeller Center
1230 Avenue of the Americas
New York, New York 10020

Designed by Quinn Hall
Manufactured in the United States of America

10   9   8   7   6   5   4   3   2   1

Library of Congress Cataloging-in-Publication Data

Mumey, Jack.
Sex and sobriety : facing the fear and building a new sexual life
/ Jack Mumey.
p.   cm. — (A Fireside/Parkside recovery book)
Includes bibliographical references and index.
1. Recovering alcoholics — Sexual behavior.   2. Recovering addicts —
Sexual behavior.   3. Sex instruction.   I. Title.   II. Series.
HV5201.S48M84   1993
362.29′13 — dc20   92-34634
                                          CIP

ISBN: 0-671-76835-2

Parkside Medical Services Corporation is a full-service provider of
treatment for alcoholism, other drug addiction, eating disorders, and
psychiatric illness.

Parkside Medical Services Corporation
205 West Touhy Avenue
Park Ridge, IL 60068
1-800-PARKSIDE

ALSO BY
JACK MUMEY

The Joy of Being Sober

Young Alcoholics

Loving an Alcoholic

Good Food for a Sober Life
(with Anne Hatcher)

Secrets in the Family

Age Different Relationships
(with Cynthia Tinsley)

While the cases described in this book are based on real people and their experiences, the author has created pseudonyms and altered identifying characteristics to preserve the privacy and anonymity of the patients and their families.

For the countless men and women who, in their recovery from the ravages of alcohol and drug abuse, have felt so frightened and alone with the prospect of reengaging in the sexual part of their world.

"Agnosco veteris vestigia flammae."
(I feel again a spark of that ancient flame.)

—VIRGIL

Contents

Contents

Preface

This book is a blueprint or a "construction schedule" for recovering persons who are hesitant and even frightened to have a new sexual, sensual, *sober* sex life.

The subject of a sober sex life comes up more often than any other among the patients I have treated in my many years as a therapist as well as among my fellow recovering men and women.

My objective here is to give you a new way to look at your relationships without the crutch of alcohol or other drugs, to help you investigate the power of commitment, the thrill of self-discovery, and the assurances of your own self-worth as a sexual and sensual partner either in a relationship or as a single person *without* those crutches.

Over and over I have heard patients express their fear of rejection, their fear of failure, and their fear of engaging in meaningful sex without the old standbys of alcohol and drugs, which probably accompanied most, if not all, of their sexual experiences before sobriety.

Sex in sobriety is different; it is awesome in its natural

power and moving in its ability to bring forth honest emotions that heretofore may have been nothing more than acting out a role.

In this book we will walk some new pathways together. I will ask you to take many risks and to reinforce your own self-worth, self-confidence, and ability to share the magnetic power of a sober yet exciting and incredibly fulfilling sexual relationship.

Don't say you've tried it all before, because you haven't. Whatever you did sexually while under the influence of drink or drugs is no longer valid. This is a new you, a sober and sane you, a person who has finally taken the pathway to recovery but still finds the exploration into sexuality risky and fearful.

In these pages you will be taught how, when, and where to make the changes that are waiting for your discovery. You will work hard, but you will be well rewarded with the outcome. I have used these techniques with many people who have stood outside in the dark corridors of their sexual fears.

Walk the path with me, learn the techniques, do the projects, explore the previously unknown power of your own sexuality. With your sobriety you have earned the chance to start a whole new life, of which your sexuality is one of the rewards and joys of being.

Acknowledgments

So many people have contributed thoughts and ideas to this book, and so many others have just plain been there when I needed them most, when my own discouragement with every writing project seemed to rise to the surface like cream on milk. I realize how important these people are.

My own staff at Gateway Treatment Center in Denver, Colorado, always bears an extra burden when I am "off writing," for it falls onto their shoulders to help pick up the caseload and handle the gaps that occur as I pour over a computer keyboard, trying to meet deadlines. They are truly remarkable and I thank them for their trust and faith in me as a writer, as well as their professional support, criticism, and general feedback on this and other projects.

My Administrative Assistant, Kimberly Costin, has made it possible for me to concentrate on writing when necessary, keeping the treatment center on line.

My new editor at Simon and Schuster in New York, Sheila Curry, has believed in this project from the beginning, and kept the book in a sharp focus, returning the manuscript to me with the challenges to "make it better"—the broad strokes and fine touches that make such a difference to any writing project. I always marvel at what such a person can do and Sheila is much appreciated by this writer.

Longtime friend and my first editor, Shari Lesser Wenk of Chicago, always seems to have time for a phone call from me. Therapist Cal Hutchins, Employee Assistance Program Denver director for United Air Lines, and an accomplished expert in sexual therapy, has always had an encouraging word. Ditto for Ms. Jennifer Elpers, LCSW, who kindly read and approved the chapter on AIDS. Clar Baskey, a distinguished colleague and friend, offered much help and encouragement on some special areas of the book.

To say my wife, Cynthia Tinsley, has been loving and helpful doesn't seem quite enough. She has read and reread with the accomplished and detached skill of her own editorial capabilities and very strong writing skills, sparing no measure to advance criticism as well as heap praise. She somehow managed to sandwich in my needs while fighting a writing monster of her own, her cherished Master of Science in Management thesis and degree from Regis University.

I have never undertaken nor completed a book project without knowing that I could count on my four adult children to encourage as well as comment on each facet of the project. The discussion of sexuality has never been a taboo subject among us, and so daughters Tracey, Dana, and Dawn from the Denver area, and son Jackson from Plantation, Florida, have always felt free to offer their opinions and encouragement, their criticisms and suggestions.

I suppose the most "raised eyebrows" about this book will come from those who, after reading some of the chapters, will invariably ask, "Have *you* done all these things *yourself*?" To them my standard reply is: "Does a mystery writer have to commit a crime to write about it?"

Thus do I protect myself and the focus of this important subject of sex and sobriety from getting lost in a personal foray into my own life. As a recovering alcoholic and a ther-

apist, I *do* attest to the importance of the subject and that I have dealt with far too many people who have to run away from the problems instead of squaring and solve them.

By picking up this book and opening its page reader, have expressed your desire to stop runni doing something about conquering your fears briety.

Go for it!

One

The Alcohol and Sex Connection

"I don't think I can *do* it anymore!"

"I feel like I'm going to fail if it ever gets that far between us."

"Frankly, I'm scared to even try to make love."

"Is it always going to be this difficult; I mean without booze?"

It was statements like these, or variations on the same theme, from dozens and dozens of my patients over the years that first got me started on this book. Were the sex lives of the men and women who were entering recovery from drinking and/or drugging going to be different?

Of course they were. Radically different. And they were going to need a new way to look at this aspect of their lives as well as the other changes that they were going to be asked to make as they progressed down the road to lifelong recovery.

The link between our sexual performance and the use of alcohol and other drugs has been well known for many years. Most people probably had their first sexual experiences while using some sort of alcohol or other drug.

Think of your own first sexual fumbling, perhaps in the backseat of the family car, the awkward yet "torrid" moves and heavy petting that you may have engaged in after you had a beer or two or a drag or more from a joint of marijuana. It is even likely that alcohol or drug use had been carefully planned as a means to allow you to engage in sexual activity.

When I looked for books on sex and sobriety I found much clinical material, but as a recovering alcoholic myself, I knew that what was really needed was a new way to look at one's sexual life, a new path on which to walk, a new and exciting world to explore with one's partner or as a single person—all without the use of alcohol or other drugs.

That's why you are reading this book now. In the bibliography I have included the cream of the crop of the clinical and quasi-clinical books and films that I think can be of value to the person wishing to expand the sexual horizons of a sober and drug-free life.

This book will explore some specific techniques and ways that you can, if you will expand your thinking and take a few risks, reach a stage of what the Japanese call the state of the "the rain and the clouds"; a poetic description of climax in sexual activity.

In order to get to what you must do, it's necessary, quite naturally, to know where you have been, and to explore the link between alcohol, drugs, and sex as you have known it in the past.

DOPAMINE, THE GREAT INHIBITOR

There is no polite way to put it; we need a "policeman" in our brain to keep us in control when it's necessary to be in control. Dopamine is that policeman.

Now, take a few drinks, or smoke some dope, or do a line of coke and what happens to the policeman? He or she goes "off-duty." The alcohol or the marijuana or the cocaine effectively knock the inhibitor out of the picture and you are free to do things you might not normally do if you were substance-free.

I suggest to my patients that dopamine is like one plug in a complicated switchboard in the brain. When alcohol or some other drug enters the system, the dopamine plug gets pulled and the circuit is broken, or disturbed, and the behavior of the drinking or drugging individual changes.

Think of your own sexual experiences, think of how much more comfortable you felt after a few drinks in even telling a dirty joke or making sexual advances toward someone you barely knew.

Think of how the first few drags of a joint or the first rush of a line of coke made you feel sexually invincible; your prowess clearly sharpened (so you believed) and thus your fear of failure in bed was practically nil. The wine, the martini, the dope, and the cocaine took the "edge" off things, didn't they?

These feelings of sexual power were merely the alcohol or drugs giving the policeman in your brain the night off; there was little or nothing to inhibit your actions, your thoughts, or your conscience.

THE SEX AND ALCOHOL CONNECTION

For centuries men have been using alcohol to help them prove their sexual prowess, and to lay claim to their masculinity as well. What these men have actually been doing is using alcohol to help them mask the anxieties and fears of failure that may have cropped up in previous sexual encounters.

Most men and women that we see in our Gateway Treatment Center are representative of men and women everywhere; they have been using alcohol or some other drug to mask their feelings or to medicate their feelings. It stands to reason, then, that if this is how one is using alcohol or drugs, then when the alcohol and drugs are taken away, the fears, failure anxieties, and all the other old demons return in full force.

So when a man or woman is drinking, alcohol can deliver a knockout blow to their dopamine and, in doing so, knock out their anxieties about sex. However, this knockout punch is only temporary, and as the alcohol or drug wears off, more needs to be consumed to keep dopamine suppressed.

PROBLEMS CAUSED BY ALCOHOL

Problems always occur when people increase their consumption of alcohol because their ability to perform begins to disappear along with their anxieties—a result of the depressant qualities of the alcohol. The use of alcohol or other drugs may have become the main reason sexual conquests were happening; the sense of sexual invincibility was a false one that was never addressed.

Now that sobriety has come into their lives, those old inhibitions are back and they're stronger than ever. There is a real possibility that the guy who thought he was God's gift in bed finds himself, now that there is no booze or pill to boost him, meek, timid, afraid, and, most of all, *unwilling* to risk the rejection that is sure to come from his awkward attempts at sexual encounters and love-play.

Women are certainly no better off. We know that the relationship between female sexuality and alcohol use is even more complex than with men. There is limited evidence that shows that alcohol directly affects the physiological mechanisms of female excitement and orgasm. Too much alcohol and females get in trouble in a different way. As reported by psychologist Dr. Michael S. Davidson a few years ago, "studies show that alcohol is a 'gonadal toxin' and therefore may inhibit a woman's ability to have sexual intercourse."

Yet women who suffer from vaginismus, a condition in which the vaginal walls are so tightly compressed as to make intercourse painful or impossible, are often helped through this dysfunction by the limited use of alcohol, which relaxes them and removes much of their inhibition.

Alcohol is a two-edged sword with sex as with everything else. Clinical evidence shows that 70–90 percent of female alcoholics who enter therapy report not being able to have orgasms, even though they reported being able to have them in the past, before their alcoholism became manifest.

"Some alcoholic women even stop having periods when drinking and others have problems with infertility and sterility," reports Dr. Davidson. In the truly alcoholic male and female we have clinical evidence that supports the statement that 50 percent of the men and 25 percent of the women have disturbances of their sexuality; all due to their alcoholism.

Men face the loss or slowing down of their testosterone production, the male hormone created in the testicles and used to keep the male libido (sex drive) high and functioning. These same men may suffer from the inability to get or maintain an erection, and/or they may suffer organic brain damage, which certainly contributes to their lack of ability to continue to perform sexually.

PROBLEMS THAT ALCOHOL MASKS

Clearly, the relationship between use of alcohol and the ability to engage in some sexual act that is distasteful or difficult, for example oral sex, has been long established. Many couples in sobriety tell me that they are "disappointed" because one or the other partner no longer wants oral sex now that they don't drink.

"She used to really dig it," he says.

"I find it vulgar, unclean, and a definite turn-off," she counters.

"You *used* to think it was the greatest, what happened?" he asks.

"That was when I had a couple of drinks and I didn't have to *think* about it," she replies.

Here is a clear example of the use of alcohol to overcome

or medicate an anxiety that has always been present for this woman. Take away the bottle, back comes the anxiety.

A recent national survey of the sexual experiences and sexual dysfunctions of Americans turned up some interesting data. Most women drinkers reported that drinking alcohol was an aphrodisiac for them; not only lessening inhibitions but allowing them a certain "closeness" with their partners that they didn't feel otherwise.

So what happens when these women stop drinking? They revert to their preexisting conditions and behaviors around their sexual beliefs and practices; the inhibitions come back and they refuse to "play games" anymore.

It's important to understand that many or even most sexual dysfunctions of a psychological nature were present *before* the individual began to use alcohol or drugs. When these people started using, they blocked the dopamine inhibitor, thus overcoming, at least temporarily, whatever bothered them about sex—whether it was oral sex, mutual or self-masturbation, "French" kissing, fondling, "dry fucking," or any number of sexual activities.

All sexual problems, regardless how big or small, were masked by the alcohol or drug consumption, and without a new look at sexuality, without a new method of building sexual relationships, the recovering abuser will undoubtedly revert to being the victim of the same fears, anxieties, and phobias that clouded sexual activities before the use of alcohol or other drugs began.

WHAT DO I DO?

Men and women have proven that their use of alcohol or drugs temporarily increases their sexual responses and feelings. You have probably been drinking or drugging to overcoming anxieties about performance, rejection, commitment, erection, orgasm—just to name a few. In sobriety, you find yourself on the receiving end of the "damned if you do, damned if you don't" equation. You've stopped drinking and

drugging and you are confronted with the anxieties you tried
to drink away.

Well, take heart. You are not unique. It is so common to
feel caught in this trap of "give up the booze, give up the
sex," that I wanted to share some practical ways to help you
give birth to your *new* sexual life whether you're single or in
a relationship, whether your male, female, straight, gay, lesbian, bisexual, young, or old. It makes no difference; the
premise is the same.

In the coming chapters you will learn how to change
your approach to sexual enjoyment, understanding, and
practice *without* returning to alcohol and drug use. That is,
after all, the real name of this game of sobriety and drug-free
living, isn't it? To be *excited* about living a life that is not
focused on injesting a chemical that alters the real you and
makes you lose control of your life.

You need to have a real understanding of what is expected of you. I am going to ask, *insist* really, that you make
changes and take risks. But these risks will not be life threatening; rather, they will help you to throw away how you've
observed things in your life before recovery, and to put into
use new ways to observe and plan, and then to *act* on those
new ways to make dramatic changes in your sexual life!

Consider this. Before sobriety, you were stumbling
through the snarled, tangled, dense underbrush of the sexual
jungle, unsure of where the next step would lead you and
whether the bridge you had to cross would safely hold and
transport you to where you were destined to go.

As you read through this book, you will be instructed on
how to walk on a new path. You will learn how to build a
new bridge to a relationship under which no water has yet
run. In so doing, you will be urged to think about your
sexuality differently. You will play games, make videos, dress
up, undress, touch, kiss, fondle, massage, caress, share — in
short, learn a new way in which your sobriety and your state
of drug-free living can catapult you into truly erotic, sensual,
pleasurable, *naturally exotic* states of sexual fulfillment with-

out the guilt, fear, anxiety, remorse, and shame that filled your days and nights when sexual activities were drowned and basted with alcohol, drugs, and uncaring, selfish behavior.

Want to try and build this new bridge? Make these changes? Take these risks? Then this book is for you.

Two

Rejection: Facing It, Conquering It

Rejection by any other name is still rejection, and that's what is to be avoided at all costs. Nobody likes being rejected; nobody wants to experience rejection as a way of life. But think about this. How many times have you wanted to have "just one little drink," one "hit off the pipe," or do "just *one* line" in order to ease the fear of a sexual encounter? And of course if, somehow, you *didn't* use and therefore were unable to overcome the fear, you faced possible rejection. Does any of that sound familiar?

Remember this. Just because you sidled up to a bar stool and got yourself half-oiled didn't make you a better sexual partner; it simply made you stop feeling a lot of the things that may have been roadblocks to sex for you. The basic you has always been there, and so it is possible for you to regain your "bar courage" without having to go to the bar.

You were probably rejected when you were actively drinking; the booze simply enabled you to shrug off the rejection and try again. The way to overcome the fear of rejection is to understand that you have a choice. You can take a risk of being rejected by a potential partner, or you can be the one who does the rejecting.

Or, if you want to let the fear of being rejected by someone rule your actions, then you can remain alone. This is a perfectly viable option, and what you have to decide is whether you want to risk being rejected or whether you want to continue to spend time alone, without a sexual partner.

Overcoming fear involves, first of all, acknowledgment of the fear. When you put a name to fear, when you openly acknowledge what it is that frightens you, then the fear begins to go away. The white knuckled air traveler is far better off telling his seat mate, the flight attendant, the ticket agent, or whomever about being afraid to fly. Getting the fear out in the open takes away much of the stranglehold that fear has on your throat.

STOP THE PUT-DOWN

What's really happening is that you believe you aren't really worth anyone's attention. You're not drinking or drugging anymore, so it may seem as if you automatically lost all the glamour, charm, general wittiness, and seductiveness that made you an object of desire. What you haven't lost is the essence of the real you, the part that makes you capable of a sexual relationship.

You are a person who is *worthwhile* to meet, to know, to love, to engage with sensually and sexually. The basic you hasn't disappeared just because the drinking or drugging behavior has stopped. You are undoubtedly a person who someone would be fortunate to get to know, both personally and sexually.

Would you like to stop putting yourself down, stop setting yourself up for rejection with all that negative thinking? You may not remember, but the alcohol you consumed didn't guarantee that you would never get rejected, it simply buffered the effect the rejection had on you.

If the real you is still worthy and capable of a sexual

encounter, then your *sobriety* makes you even that much more attractive and desirable, because you will know what's taking place this time.

Now what in the world makes that so scary? One of the principal reasons you entered recovery in the first place was so you could take control of your life again, so you could honestly feel elation, joy, and yes, even pain, and you wanted to experience the *living* of your life without artificial means.

This is your chance to overcome your fear of rejection by believing yourself worthy of having a relationship. Look at it this way. Maybe you weren't ready to have a relationship before, but now, in sobriety, you are. Isn't the promise of a healthy relationship exciting enough to make you stop putting yourself down, to believe that you can and *will* engage in a meaningful sexual relationship without fear and without drugs?

Part of the fear of rejection is based on your belief that people won't like you or want you if you are in control of your sexual feelings. Maybe all your life you have played an emotional tape that told you, "Let other people be in control, then they'll want you!" By following this tape you are giving someone else power over your life. When you give up that power—whether to another individual or to something like alcohol or other drugs—you become an onlooker in the game of life, not a player.

THE NEW YOU

At first, being comfortable with the new you may not be easy; in fact, it may be downright uncomfortable, because you're not used to being in charge of your own life, your own feelings. But if you are going to take the necessary risks that change requires, then you need to practice how it can be with the new you, the person who is *unafraid* of rejection.

Look back on your childhood. Were you in mortal fear of not being chosen for that game of stickball? Could anything have been worse than not being picked? One by one the other kids were selected until finally someone *had* to take you.

You could have died of embarrassment and hurt, angry that you have never shown the other kids that you had the right stuff to be on their team. You may have reacted by simply not being there the next time someone wanted to get up a game. Well, that would fix them, wouldn't it? If you weren't there, they couldn't reject you, could they?

So you chose not to participate. And here you are now, all grown up and possibly behaving the same way. Making yourself unavailable so you won't have the embarrassment, the humiliation, of not being selected, of being rejected. What an awful way to live!

The new you has got to get right in there and change that negative thinking. What you need to say now is, "Anyone would be damn lucky to have me as a partner for whatever it is we are going to do." Say it and mean it.

WHAT GOES TOGETHER

Another experience from the past may have you believing that alcohol or some other drug and sex go together. Well, get rid of that idea because it's not true. What goes together are men and women, or same-sex partners if you are gay or lesbian, but *not* sex and alcohol.

Remember that the more you drank, the *less* you were able to engage in satisfying and rewarding sex, even though you own experience had been to use alcohol to have "better sex." Let's explore this a little further. You probably started out using alcohol to enhance the event, but because you are an alcoholic or another kind of substance abuser, you began to build a need, an addiction, for the chemical itself, rather than as an adjunct to sexual gratification.

You helped create you own double addiction. You were already addicted to the chemical, and then you tied in the use of that chemical to the engagement of sex, and there you are;

unable, or mostly unwilling, to even try sexual activity without the drug.

With that kind of double addiction is it any wonder that you feared sexual encounters without your crutch? You need to realize that you never started out with the need for the chemical and it's relation to "great" sex. You created that need every time you tied the two together, then you began to increase your use of the alcohol or the drug—quite possibly to the point that sex was a downright *failure* because of your alcohol use.

Therefore, something *you* created, *you* can destroy! Break the connection between the use of alcohol or other drugs and sex, and you have won most of the battle of the fear of rejection.

THE POSITIVE APPROACH

Almost every self-help program, every self-help book that I've ever read speaks of the need for a positive attitude. But it's very hard to have or maintain such an attitude when you are constantly getting emotionally "beat up" through rejection. It's quite possible that you just say over and over, "What's wrong with me? Why do I keep getting turned down?"

In a positive approach, I believe you have to abandon the old ways of doing things. They are not going to work anymore—if they ever did. I tell my patients, particularly those in relationship counseling, that we will not look at how things are between them now. You see, we know that things between them now are terrible, otherwise they wouldn't be sitting in my office. I tell them that we will look instead at how things *can* be between them and what steps must be taken for them to arrive at where they want the relationship to be.

It's exactly the same with you. Your new you and your positive approach about fear and rejection is to say, "I don't care how it was before. I want to look ahead to how it can be." In other words, you must picture yourself as not being rejected. You must see yourself as a successful player despite what might have happened in the past. It doesn't matter that as a child you weren't chosen for sandlot softball. What matters now is that you see yourself as being chosen.

Visualize yourself as the person who has a great deal to offer someone, so much, in fact, that they will be very fortunate to recognize it. Are we simply playing mind games here? Are we just painting some rosy-red view of how it really is out there in single's land or in a now-sober relationship? Experience tells me "no." Working with so many patients over the years has reinforced the belief that the ability to *visualize*, the ability to *see* oneself as being successful, is a big step toward arriving at those goals.

When I say "successful," I am referring to your ability to engage in sexual activities and nurture a relationship without having to return to the use of alcohol or some other drug.

REINFORCING YOURSELF

Go stand in front of your full-length mirror. Naked. Look at yourself and be critical. Sure, maybe there's a flabby area or two, maybe your breasts aren't as big as you think they should be. Maybe your penis remains "infinitesimal" in your estimation. Perhaps your hair has thinned or your legs aren't as shapely as you would like. Is there a paunch? Does your tummy or butt need a "tuck"?

Maybe yes, maybe no. One thing that you must know for certain, if there are flaws (and doesn't everyone have some?), do you think they weren't there before, when you were drinking? They may have been more pronounced then than they are now, because drinking and drugging takes such a toll on your body and your health.

So take another look, and take a stab at some positive statements about yourself. "I'm worth a relationship!" is a good phrase to start with. "Someone ought to feel lucky to have a relationship with me or to know me sexually." As you lengthen your sobriety, you will notice that you no longer show the ravages of alcohol and drug abuse, the baggy eyes, the flabby face, the red-veined nose, or the light gray skin color that besieged you in those awful days. You can begin to look to how things can be instead of how they are.

The new you will not recognize rejection nor the fear of it anymore. That was how you *used* to do things. A glance at how it can be for you, tells you that you will *not* be rejected forever, even though you may not be chosen right away. The attitude you now have says that eventually you *will* be chosen and you will make choices and therefore you need have no fear.

You may begin to notice that you are now wearing more flattering and perhaps more colorful, youthful-looking clothes. You are no longer putting thousands of unwanted and unhealthy calories into your body through alcohol, so your clothes will look better, fit better, *be* better and help show the new you in a more positive package.

Men who have been so fearful of being rejected by women can begin to think of themselves and to see themselves as *not* being rejected when, for example, they ask someone to dance. That doesn't mean that every woman in the place is going to want to dance with you, but it does mean that *somewhere* in that place there is a woman who *will* dance with you, because that's probably why *she's* there. You just need to keep asking.

If you are a woman who never gets asked to dance, then look at the future. Ask yourself, "What do I want it to be like? What do I need to do to get to what I want it to be? Do I need to look a little less unapproachable? Do I need to see what my competition (the ones who *are* being asked) is doing?"

All of these questions and others that you ask yourself are designed to have you picture the scenario the way you want it to be—namely, a partner asking you to dance and your accepting the invitation. I don't care how it *has* been—that was in the past. Always look at how it *can* be.

Fear of rejection is a waste of time and energy. You could even use the fear as a means of relapsing into alcohol or drug use. Obviously, you must not let that happen. Your sobriety or your remaining drug free is your *number one priority*. Returning to that "one little drink," that "one small hit" so as to face possible rejection gives away all your power again.

STOP PROJECTING FAILURE

Don't project what might happen sexually. Instead, feel good enough about yourself that you consider yourself worthy of being attractive to someone else and also being ready to have a relationship or a sexual encounter.

"I deserve respect and I'm also entitled to your attention" may sound a little on the egocentric side, but that's okay. You deserve it. My reason for giving you these thoughts is so you will change your negative, fear-inducing thinking into positive vibes that say, "You [the prospective partner] just might deserve to know [and love] me. And if you play your cards right, you might get the chance."

In short, don't project failure. Begin with the premise that it will be *you* who does the choosing, and not the other way around. This may seem to be just another way of setting yourself up for failure, but let me remind you of something: When you were drinking or drugging, it was the chemical that was making all the moves, not the real you at all, and that's false. To put it even stronger, try this out on yourself: "Since nobody really knew me except when I was drinking, they never got the chance to know the real me . . . they had to accept or reject a false image that was enhanced by alcohol or dope. Since the *real* me never got rejected (only the alcohol/drug me), then what do I have to lose if I now present the real me?"

I can hear you readers groaning all the way across the

country. "Oh, sure, the *real* me, huh? The real me couldn't ever smile, or be witty, or be seductive or say bright and charming things, or tell good jokes, or . . ."

Hold it, please! I suggest that you probably never tried to do any of these things in sobriety. You took the easy, the lazy, the *alcoholic* or doper way out.

Of course, you still run the risk of rejection. I won't gloss that over because it's part of the dating game, or any other game for that matter. However, you've a better than even chance that you won't fail, because you are now in control of yourself. You have taken back the power over your life that you gave to alcohol or drugs; you have assumed command again, and the real you, the new you, is able to handle rejection and is also able to release yourself from the fear of rejection.

You are going to take the risk of trying to see things as they can be for you, taking the necessary steps to get there, and you are *not* going to use fear or the fear of being rejected as an excuse to return to the old ways of drinking and drugging. You have much to gain and as we proceed through these chapters together, much to stimulate you to take action for happy, healthy, and fulfilling change.

Three

Performance Anxiety

"God, what if I can't do it?"

"How will I ever get over these shaky feelings?"

"What if I can't keep an erection?"

"Can I ever have an orgasm again?"

Performance anxiety. The pressure to perform while engaging in any act of sexuality is very intense. Everyone knows that and it really doesn't matter whether you are in recovery or have been a teetotaler; it's still there, hidden in the not-too-deep recesses of your brain.

This pressure is almost unbearable. Admit it. Most of that performance pressure is self-applied, so no wonder that, in the past, a little drink or two, or perhaps a hit off a joint, took the edge off this fear. When you were using it was possible to think of sexual success instead of failure, and this is an important point to relearn.

THE PRESSURE TO PERFORM TEST

This is not a "pass-fail" thing; no points are given for "correct" answers, or demerits for "wrong" answers. Instead, just write down your responses to these questions about your performance anxiety.

Don't just answer with a simple "yes" or "no." You won't learn anything unless you are willing to make a little extra effort for yourself. As you write down your answers, you will probably find yourself free associating with many of the performance anxieties that have been building up in you over time. As you come across possible solutions to these anxieties, write them down on a separate page labeled "Solutions."

While you take this little quiz, keep telling yourself: "I have performance anxieties because I am no longer using alcohol or drugs to mask them. All of my fears are *learned* fears, so they can be *unlearned* as well."

Further, say out loud, even if there is someone around who can hear you: "I am the same person I was when I engaged in sex before; what's different and exciting and wonderful *now* is that I will feel and truly delight in the experiences of passion, *without* the false high I got from my drinking and/or drugging."

1. Do I believe I'm just as "good" sexually as before?
2. Are there things I don't want to do (sexually) now that I did before?
3. Do I believe my partner is happy with our sex life now?
4. Am I dreading sexual encounters now that I'm in recovery?
5. As I making excuses not to do things sexually out of fear of not living up to his/her expectations?
6. Have I set such lofty standards for myself as "punishment" for my past alcohol/drug use?
7. Do I believe my performance anxieties are caused by guilt that I was so sexually "different" when I was drinking/using?
8. Do I fear losing my partner because I'm not as "good" now?

9. Am I really afraid to let go in my sexual expressions because he/she always thought it was my alcohol/drug that made me act with such "wild" abandon?

10. Am I afraid that sex will never be the same for me again?

Remember to write down answers; don't just say "yes" or "no." Feel free to alter your answers as you continue to read through this chapter, and above all, treat the answers as possible "Solutions."

SELF-INDUCED PRESSURE

Most of the pressure one feels around sex comes from within and not your partner. Of course, that doesn't mean that your partner might not absolutely devastate you after sex with some caustic remark that makes you feel like the world's biggest failure. However, by and large, *you* are the one who applies most of the sexual pressure by wanting sex to be "the best," "the longest," or the "most orgasmic."

Whatever the pressures, chances are there's a lot of lying involved in the exchange between the partners over performance. A 1990 Lou Harris and Associates poll commissioned by *Men's Health* magazine revealed that only 12 percent of men and 8 percent of women believe their lovers are telling the truth all the time about their sexual experiences.

What this implies is that you might be building a "portfolio" for yourself and then forcing yourself to perform sexually with an eye toward living up to your own "reviews." This is a sure path to failure since very few people always meet the high expectations they set for themselves in *any* endeavor of their lives.

The Harris poll focused on telephone interviews with 1,250 adults who essentially told the interviewers that there was a "gray area of honesty" (my words) about sexual experiences. This gray area must exist, for 22 percent of men and 28 percent of the women in the sample told the Harris researchers that they thought they were getting the whole truth from their sexual partners "only occasionally."

Is it not possible, then, that what you might have been doing is "beefing up" your own performance stats so that when you do go "on stage" so to speak (with a sexual performance), you try to live up to your own advance billing?

Sir Laurence Olivier, certainly one of the greatest actors of our or anyone's time, suffered inexplicably from stage fright. But he also suffered from another kind of "stage fright," that of sexual performance. Olivier wrote in his autobiography: "My prowess, so often failing from *nervous* premature ejaculation, had gained, through the practice given to me by my gently, kindly, patiently bestowed few love affairs, a calmly confident strength. . . ."

Sir Laurence was referring to his attempts to rekindle the passion between himself and his estranged wife, actress Vivien Leigh. He was, quite candidly, attributing his ability to conquer sexual dysfunction to his extramarital liaisons. This isn't the best solution today. In this age of the AIDS epidemic, casual, devil-may-care sex with multiple partners becomes not only irresponsible but deadly. You need to try something different now that having affairs has taken on sinister reprisals.

ALCOHOL HELPED

There's no point in denying it; alcohol helped ease your performance anxiety. It temporarily blocked the possibilities of failure and overcame the inhibitions that might have been the stumbling blocks to your "sexual success."

In other words, in the past, the "stage fright" generated by your sexual performance had been handled in a different way; you simply had a few drinks to deaden those inhibitions, allowing you to be the "wild and passionate" person that lives within your fantasies.

Unfortunately, without your inhibitions, you may have given yourself a pretty big buildup to your current or long-term love partner. In sobriety, with the prop of alcohol removed, you have to deal with the terror that may have taken its place.

That's absolutely no way to live. It's surely no way to have satisfying, rich, and rewarding sex.

THE HONESTY CONNECTION

When you were using alcohol or some other drug, more often than not you believed you were living up to your billing. The alcohol or the drug really didn't allow you to feel much of anything because of the anesthetizing effect of those chemicals. What the alcohol *did* do was help you overcome what may have been some natural fear of certain things about sex. Thus, while using, you were able to perform with starlike quality.

Now it's time for the "honesty connection," a way to bring back honesty and the need for you to verbalize your fears to your partner, therefore initiating a whole new approach to sexual behavior.

I have learned from working with hundreds of recovering alcoholics that when the basics of honesty are practiced, the rewards are great. In case after case, when I have encouraged patients to "tell the truth" and to share the "agony and the fear" about sex, they report back to me that their partner also confessed some fear of his or her own. Result? They started sharing these fears, began honestly communicating with each other, and their sexual relationships became rewarding and fun, and not the least bit fearful.

Many men, new to sobriety, have a lessened interest in sex for a while. This is partly due to their rebuilding low testosterone levels that were depleted during their drinking days. It is also a result of their having convinced themselves that they can't possibly perform sexually without their old standby, booze.

Talking this out, *trying* it out, will improve that state of mind.

Women, perhaps already burdened by many years of feeling sexually inadequate, of blocking those fears by drinking or using other drugs, now face sobriety and being clean and straight with the same fears they harbored before. Talking them out with your partners can help erase those fears. Knowing there is no such thing as being inadequate, but only perhaps unskilled, can give new hope; skills can be taught and learned.

TAKING OFF THE PRESSURE

By taking the pressure off yourself to live up to what may have been a sexual lie, you will be able to relax and naturally investigate with your partner the wonderful and fulfilling world of sex and sobriety; this time actually *feeling* the experiences of sex.

It's still going to be a difficult process—taking the pressure off and telling the truth—but the rewards are many. After all, telling your partner that you're really terrified to have sexual intercourse because "I can't remember the last time I did without being half smashed," requires a good deal of personal risk.

But verbalizing that anxiety can help make it disappear. When you have identified a specific anxiety and talked about it, it begins to lose its power over you. For example, oral sex may have been a real pressure situation for you. When you were drinking, you might have just tolerated it. The anxieties about the act itself, the smell, taste, touch, fear of swallowing ejaculate or vaginal fluids were all numbed by the alcohol.

Your senses of taste and smell were actually dulled by the booze because your body's natural supply of zinc was used up by the drinking. Zinc is needed for better eyesight, the healing of wounds, the production of sperm, and the heightened sense of taste and smell. When you drank, the zinc was not available for any of those things because it was used by the ninety-two enzymes that your body pressed into action to detoxify the alcohol you consumed.

So now, in sobriety, all of your senses are sharpened; so
much improved, in fact, that you are experiencing a lot of
anxiety about the act of oral sex. You'll not have the alcohol
buffer to work for you. By being honest and communicating
your anxiety to your partner, you can overcome your anxiety. You can also relearn your approach to sex.

SEX IS A LEARNED SKILL

Drs. Masters and Johnson have taught that sex as a learned
skill can be a most rewarding adventure. It stands to reason
then that if you can be introduced to sexual *techniques*, then
your anxieties about being "clumsy" or inadequate can van-
ish. You can go "on stage" with stellar performances almost
every time.

If you are an alcoholic, you are most probably a Type-A
obsessive-compulsive personality. Dr. Joseph LoPiccolo, a
distinguished sex researcher at the State University of New
York, Stony Brook, has said that obsessive-compulsive people sometimes get stuck with "terminal prissiness."

Fear of ejaculation in the mouth or the taste of vaginal
fluids are certainly heightened by this "prissiness" and
"messiness" attitude. Dr. LoPiccolo told a Minneapolis
workshop audience I attended that "obsessive-compulsive
people often find that sex is just too messy for them."

It makes sense, then, that you must learn to overcome
this anxiety by learning new techniques and skills that will
overcome your natural "prissiness." And it can be done without having to revert to alcohol as you did before.

There is nothing inherently wrong with you, you have
just never dealt with these anxieties in a sober state. You
simply "drank through them." For example, men may develop a severe aversion to the smell of the vagina, but when
drinking, the smell of their own alcohol, plus the numbing
effect of the sense of smell, make vaginal contact tolerable.

Without the alcohol, the sense of smell becomes heightened by the body's better use of zinc, and you may have a

sexually dysfunctionate male who cannot even get *close* to a vagina. One technique we may try is dabbing his partner's favorite perfume around the vaginal area to help overcome his aversion. This is a learned skill.

Teach a woman through the "systems therapy" espoused by Dr. LoPiccolo and his colleagues to control male ejaculation through the "pause and squeeze" technique, and you soon have a woman who no longer has anxiety about "giving head" for fear of sperm suddenly being ejaculated into her mouth. At the same time, it will also help a man overcome the anxieties of premature ejaculation.

Techniques and learned skills *can* work to overcome the pressure to perform.

TALKING IS IMPORTANT

I keep urging you to talk about your anxieties with your partner. Telling him or her that you have never been able to do this or that without drinking or drugging is not admitting that you are a failure. Quite the contrary; it means that you have been *afraid* to fail. Your performance anxiety has always been so high that you could not and would not risk having sex without drinking or drugging to bolster your courage and help you overcome your anxieties.

Believe it or not, talking about sex is, in itself, a turn on for many couples. Revealing what you think and feel about sex can reveal your vulnerability and not only heighten your closeness but you may learn you share some of the same fears.

This can lead to an ultimate in sexual experiences; the ones that occur when you say, "maybe we can help each other. We *can* help each other lose this anxiety performance." Nobody is going to grade your performance. There is no pass/fail system at work here except what you yourself have put into play.

It's helpful to remember that the pressure to perform and the fear of the failure to perform are closely allied; they both come down to your belief that if you are a poor sex partner you stand to lose this relationship. So you continue to grit your teeth and do the things that you hate sexually, unable to drink away the fears that engulf you, all because you fear the loss of your partner. Talking together, the fun of experimentation of what will work for you both and what doesn't, the teaching and learning of each other's desires and wants, and the things that were rarely a part of your drinking sex life can now come about by working together.

Once you understand and believe that you have been your own worst enemy, demanding performance from yourself instead of looking toward mutually satisfying, unselfish sharing of your sexuality, then you are well on your way to overcoming the "stage fright" that has been afflicting you since you entered sobriety.

Talking about sexual expectations can help you both set those expectations aside. In other words, your partner might be the very one to say to you, "Hey, don't worry about whether I have an orgasm or not. I'm responsible for my own orgasm. What I want with you is the sharing of the joy we can reach together." Wouldn't *that* be nice to hear or to say to the person you are with?

Four

Fear of Failure

It's easy to understand how all of your failure fears came about; you and everyone else, whether recovering or not, are a product of your life experiences. We know that your "life script," the way in which you respond psychologically, emotionally, and physically to life's problems and situations, was written when you were about four or five years old.

Think about how many of those behaviors and the responses to those behaviors have become a part of your everyday life. The way you have functioned or not functioned sexually has been a mixed bag; some of it has been terrific, but a lot of it has been uninformed, misguided, scary, and wrong.

ALCOHOL AND DRUGS: THE RESCUERS

Alcohol, or maybe marijuana, cocaine, or prescription drugs of one kind or another, seemed like knights in shining armor that came charging into your sex life to vanquish all the demons that you had hiding there for years.

It's good to remember that these knights were part of your fantasy; you created them. The fears that accompanied these fantasies were also created by you, and can just as easily be put to rest. Your fears are not unique; countless thousands of other men and women have had them, plus some that you haven't had. Therefore, you are not alone in this sea of fear.

But what are these fears, at least the most common? Experience tells us that there are some specific fears shared by most of you, but they could all be covered under a massive umbrella of thought that says: "I am afraid to experience (sexual) things without the crutch of alcohol (or other drugs), because I don't think I can perform."

Any fears you had before you started using alcohol or some other drug were temporarily taken away by your chemical use. The chemical helped to numb the fear or helped you to ignore the fear and the anxiety it caused. So now, in sobriety, that fear and anxiety could return, couldn't it?

Then there is the fear that in a sober state you might fail at whatever you are doing sexually. You no longer have the drug to mask that fear.

SPECIFIC FEARS

I mentioned anxiety and fear earlier. The fear of failure in sex and the anxiety caused by the pressure to perform are closely linked. It's difficult to experience one without the other, and in fact, you probably don't have a failure fear that is not anxiety producing.

Here are some specific fears that you may not have verbalized, either to yourself or to your partner. Yet they may be a part of your life script, and without the crutch of alcohol or drug use, they may become manifest. These fears could include:

Failing to have an erection.
Failing to maintain an erection.

Failing to have an orgasm.
Failing to have intercourse at all because it's too painful.
Failing to provide pleasure to your partner.
Failing to have successful foreplay.
Failing to overcome the "guilt" of sex.
Failing to delay ejaculation.
Failing to ejaculate at all.

This is by no means the definitive list of such fears. Your own list can be added to or taken from those above. Actually, it would be a good idea for you to write down just such a list so that you can at least get the specific fears out of your mind and down on paper.

Like all fears, once they are spoken or written, they begin to lose their punch, because you are no longer hiding them deep inside, allowing them to have control over your feelings. So go ahead and add the very special fears that only you know about and understand.

A SPECIAL FEAR

One special fear that is almost universal in recovering people is that they believe they have lost their ability to be sensual and sexual. When drinking, you were probably told countless times that you were sexy and slinky and debonair and experienced and suave and cool and so on.

Now that you have entered a life of sobriety, you have this gnawing, deep fear that you are no longer as sexy, slinky, debonair, and so on as when you were drinking. Know what happens? You believe this to be true so you don't even try to be any of those things. It's as if the alcohol was responsible for casting you in all those roles, and without the drinking you couldn't possibly live up to your advance billing.

The fear becomes so ingrained that you begin doing crazy things, like never wearing that dynamite dress you used to wear, or the tie and suspenders outfit that always made you feel good about yourself.

You don't do your hair with a blow dryer anymore or wear the color nail polish that always seemed to elicit comments from male companions. In short, you stopped making an effort with your appearance; stopped doing the things that gave you a confident and assured look and feeling when you were going to be with a sexual partner.

BEGINNING TO OVERCOME FEAR

It's time to make changes. Get out those great-looking clothes and attitudes that you used when you were drinking. After all, the fear of failure is born out of your possibly never having any kind of sex without alcohol being a part of it; so naturally you think that your drama will "bomb in Boston."

If you really look deep into your heart and soul, you will own up to this truth, and you certainly won't be alone. Most adults have never had sexual experiences from the very first without some kind of stimulant, some kind of sedative, some kind of booster or other artificial "aid" to help them over the fear of a sexual encounter.

As you went on in life, maybe it just became habit for you to have that drink or two, that joint or two, that line of cocaine, before you could really feel the sex!

Now that you are in recovery, it makes perfect sense to believe that you will fail unless you use what you had always used to prepare for the sexual experience at hand.

YOUR LIFE SCRIPT AT WORK

Let's take an example from your sexual past and see how your life script called for you to perform. We'll use the example of one of the fears from my general list: premature ejaculation.

When you were drinking, this particular fear was pretty well handled. Alcohol, being a sedative drug (*not* a stimulant), enabled you to engage in intercourse for a much longer period of time than usual because you were numbed. Your inhibitions had been knocked out; you felt somewhat invincible and were able to maintain your erection for much longer than usual.

In recovery, and without the anesthetic of alcohol, you have a very real fear that you will once again be struck with premature ejaculation. It all makes perfect sense, and I would not for a moment try to discount your feelings. However, since you are committed to a life of sobriety, other ways will have to be found so that you will not be a victim of this fear any longer. In all probability, you never dealt with the cause of the problem. Alcohol was the agent that simply and *temporarily* helped you overcome it.

In the case of premature ejaculation, an early life experience with prostitutes or experience as a teenager fumbling around in the backseat of a car could well be the emotional and psychological triggers that have set off your problem.

Your life scripting goes to work and conditioning patterns are set up in childhood and carry right on into the teen years and adulthood. If you developed this premature ejaculation pattern as a result of early experiences, then the chances are you simply grew up with it, and it's always been there, masked and held in check by the alcohol, which allowed you to break out of those habit patterns and experiences from the past.

Stop drinking and what happens? The premature ejaculation patterns starts up again. No wonder you have a failure fear around this issue.

HOW IT HAPPENED

How did the pattern develop? There are a number of reasons, but look at the two examples I cited.

If you first began your sexual experiences by losing your virginity with a hooker, you probably remember that the lady was not too interested in spending a whole lot of time listening to your life story. Her job was to turn "tricks" as quickly as possible, particularly if you weren't exactly a big spender and was just being treated to a "quickie" by well-meaning friends or relatives who thought it was time for you to "get laid." You began your sexual experiences with someone who urged you to "hurry up," and hurry up you did.

Consequently, every sexual experience proved a disaster for you because you did not learn the sexual staying power that would please or certainly satisfy a partner. When more and more drink entered the picture, you then began another dependency; no booze, no good, long-lasting sex. And here you are right back to square one. Or so it seems.

If your first teenage or preteen sexual experiences happened in the backseat of a car, you were no doubt in the frame of mind that said, "God, I better hurry before we get caught!" Being parked on a dark street, or on a Lovers Lane didn't exactly guarantee that you would have all the time in the world to explore this fantastic new and strange experience.

Scared to death of being caught and of the awful punishment that was sure to await you, you "came." Not only was it premature, it was probably clumsy, messy, and in a most undistinguished fashion.

You can change the scenario to fit your own personal experiences, but I'm sure it's not much different from these examples.

TREATING THE PROBLEM (MALE)

I want to stress that it's imperative that both men and women make sure there are no purely physical problems connected with their sexual dysfunctions. Be sure to get a complete physical and discuss the problem with your doctor. If you check out physically, then its time to address possible psychological causes.

Sex therapists today use many techniques to help individuals and couples overcome sexual problems. One of the ways to treat sexual dysfunction uses so-called systems therapy, and the "pause and squeeze" method of helping to overcome premature ejaculation is most certainly in this category.

This technique was originally developed in 1959 by Dr. James Semans as a means of teaching men to delay ejaculation. Masters and Johnson modified the technique, which then became known as the "squeeze" method, and the combination of this "pause" and "squeeze" proved very effective in helping men control the timing of their ejaculation without giving up the passion and eroticism of their sexual play.

In pausing, the male stops receiving stimulation, either by himself or with his partner's help, just before he feels he will ejaculate. He then waits until this high level of arousal subsides, maybe even losing his erection, before he begins again to be stimulated.

With the renewed stimulation, his erection will no doubt return, and he will have gained the advantage of delaying ejaculation. In intercourse, he simply stops all movement until the ejaculation feeling subsides. There may, however, be an interference with his partner's building up to an orgasm, but practice will iron out the timing.

In the squeeze technique, the man or his partner applies pressure to the penis, just below the head and just before the moment when he is about to come. The thumb is placed below the head of the penis on one side with the index and middle fingers on the opposite side. Sufficient pressure is then applied to stop him from ejaculating.

The man may lose some of his erection by squeezing, but it will return as soon as stimulation is started again.

TREATING THE PROBLEM (FEMALE)

A female dysfunction from our list at the beginning of this chapter, failing to have intercourse because it's too painful, is a relatively common complaint. Let's look at it more closely and see if the fear can be effectively treated and dissolved.

Suppose that for most of the times that you have engaged in sexual intercourse, the act itself was quite painful. The vagina clamped down tightly and every thrust of your partner's penis only made you cry out in pain. This most likely was a condition called "vaginismus," often called "the great undiagnosed disorder." It is quite common in female alcoholics and contributes greatly to their continued use of alcohol as a means of simply enduring sexual intercourse. You turned more and more to the use of alcohol in order to relax yourself, to allow the vagina to relax and to make penile penetration not only possible but endurable because the pain was gone.

Now, in sobriety, the fear factor is pressing heavily on you, saying, "Without the booze I'm going back to painful intercourse." Once again, this is simply not true, or at least should not be taken as gospel. Again, it is absolutely necessary for you to see your physician to make sure that there are not physical reasons that may be generating or contributing to any of these problems.

Assuming you have a clean bill of health from your doctor, let's go on to conquer the fear. Sexual intercourse, no matter what age it first occurred, might have been a very painful experience. Certainly the loss of your virginity, either by penile penetration or by some inanimate object, by accident, or with the help of a surgeon, was probably a painful experience, and may have continued to be so. Using a lubricant such as K-Y gel may have become a regular and necessary part of sexual intercourse. However, you may have developed a psychological block to intercourse, one that constantly told you, "This pain is going to be there every time I have sex."

It's easy to understand what a welcome relief alcohol would be if it could make the pain go away, how the very act of sex became not only possible but even pleasurable by mixing passion and alcohol! The alcohol, of course, merely reduced inhibitions that enabled you to relax and allow penile penetration.

So now you are faced with the same failure fear as the man with his sexual dysfunctions. Namely, "If I don't have a drink or two to relax me, the old pain of (sex) will come back!" Rather than risking breaking your sobriety, you may have possibly just given up intercourse, and wouldn't that be a shame! To deny yourself one of life's pleasure because of fear is simply not acceptable.

Relaxation techniques, Kegel exercises, and working with dilators, are just a few of the steps systems therapy follows in treatment of vaginismus. The results are rewarding and wonderful for you, the female recovering alcoholic.

NO "FRIGIDITY" ALLOWED

You can readily see how these failure fears can be disassembled one by one, no matter what they are. You were not born dysfunctionate and "cold," "frigid," or any of those other labels that make excuses for treatable sexual problems. I like to remind my patients that "God did not make women dysfunctionate nor frigid, so you can take most of the credit for that yourself!" As a matter of fact, nearly 80 percent of the sexual problems experienced by women are psychological, with 20 percent being physical. Joe LoPiccolo made me laugh when he elaborated on that theme by saying, "Yes, there *are* frigid women and they marry incompetent men!'"

FEAR AND FAILURE ARE MAJOR PLAYERS

When we examine the sexual problems of men and women in recovery, it is amazing to discover how much fear and the failure factors have played in the dysfunction. No one blames you for having these fears. After all, you *learn* behavior, and when behaviors become reinforced, they are simply repeated.

If you are a man who has always had premature ejaculation problems, you have always been reinforced with the fears and guilt that were associated with sex from your early teenage experiences, then you simply continued to repeat the behavior of premature ejaculation. The alcohol didn't do a whole lot for the ejaculation problem except block the fears from those earlier experiences, thus breaking the reinforcement of the behavior.

What you now have to do is learn to remove those old reinforcing fears *without* the use of alcohol; substituting instead the systems and practices that will put you more in control of the timing of your ejaculations.

If you are a woman who has suffered from vaginismus and has used alcohol to overcome that problem, what you were doing was blocking the fear and pain of intercourse. Without alcohol you must learn the techniques and the systems that will enable you to really enjoy intercourse—and without the pain that has been a part of your past. It is *absolutely* possible to do this! Please trust the process and seek the kind of help that I have been offering in this chapter.

MORE FAILURE FEARS

Let's look at another sexual dysfunction or two and see how fear has played havoc with your sex life. We've talked about the problem of premature ejaculation, but what about the inability to ejaculate at all? This particular sexual dysfunction used to be called "ejaculation incompetence." A few years ago, sex researchers decided that the word *incompetence* might apply more to a skill level than to the function in sex it was describing; so they changed it, and we now refer to this dysfunction as "ejaculation inhibition."

It becomes a failure fear when you stop having, or fail to initiate or participate in, sexual activity because you just know you are going to be inhibited and not be able to ejaculate, causing embarrassment, anger, and a real sense of low self-esteem on the part of your partner; he or she being made to believe they were unable to make you come.

Once again, when you were drinking or using drugs, you lost this inhibition, and although you may not have come every time, the odds were that you did get the job done more often than not. Now, in sobriety, the old fear tape is playing again, and that's not acceptable.

What causes this inhibition to ejaculate in the first place? There are two principle reasons: (1) the fear of having a child, and (2) religious or societal taboos. Once again, I am ruling out any physical reason for ejaculation inhibition.

Fear of Having a Child

If you are terrified of becoming a parent; if the circumstances of your life are such that parenthood is simply not what you want, then your ability to ejaculate when engaged with a partner is definitely inhibited. After all, if you don't "come" how can you possibly contribute to the creation of a child?

Again, be fearless for a moment and look at your behavior when you were drinking. In that mode, you didn't give a damn about the consequences of anything you did, so it makes perfect sense that with your sobriety, the old fear of parenthood or possible parenthood returns.

This inhibition probably goes back a long way in your psychological history and very likely has been a strong factor in your inhibited ejaculation. You may have come to really enjoy and receive compliments for the great "staying power" that you manifest with your sex partner, until he or she begins to complain about the lack of completion of the act.

Even wearing a condom, something you should be doing *anyway,* has not been able to keep your failure fear from kicking in. You may believe that you have the one condom out of the whole package or even *lot* that has a hole in it! So you trust nothing that might get you into the spot of possible parenthood.

Religious or Societal Taboos

To look at this reason for the dysfunction requires that you go back to the religious beliefs that were instilled in you during your youth. In other words, were you raised in a faith that told you that almost anything in the sexual category was okay as long as you didn't have a completed act?

Think about it. When you were a little kid, and then a teenager, was it okay to "fool around," to "make out," as long as you didn't have an orgasm?

When you were "making out," maybe everything was allowed by your religious training *except* the very act of culmination—that is, the ejaculatory orgasm that might carry the sperm to a ripe egg, possibly beginning a new life. If that scenario is or was scary for you, then it's easy to see how you could allow the chains of these beliefs to inhibit your ability to ejaculate. When you turned to alcohol, the chains of fear were broken temporarily, and you didn't stop to think about what you religion *or* society was telling you; you simply did what was natural.

If you have been so instilled with these religious or societal taboos against completing the sex act with ejaculating, then you must realize those taboos probably haven't gone away while you've been busy drinking yourself to death! You have simply put a lid on them, and now that sobriety has come into your life, the lid has come off.

But there is a two-edged sword here. On one edge, you may have been using alcohol to overcome the so-called retarded ejaculation problem. But on the other edge, the more you drank, the less was your ability to achieve ejaculation because of the depression or sedation of your central nervous system by the alcohol.

This inhibited or retarded ejaculation as a failure fear could be so strong that you simply *avoid* sex altogether so as not to have to deal with the inability to ejaculate. And yet, you may find that masturbation will produce an ability to ejaculate, which is confusing. You are able to achieve orgasm when it is autoerotically induced. As soon as you are with a partner, the inhibition returns.

THE ROLE OF ALCOHOL

There is certainly much physical evidence that connects ejaculation inhibition with the use of alcohol and other drugs in
the first place; particularly in the case of the person who is
clearly alcoholic. However, these folks may have no such
inhibited ejaculation *until* the alcohol is playing an important
role in their sex lives.

A valued friend and professional colleague, Dr. Gary
Forrest, a licensed clinical psychologist and executive director of Psychotherapy Associates, P.C., has written an important clinical work, *Alcoholism and Human Sexuality*, first
published in 1983. In it he writes: "Such patients usually
indicate that retarded ejaculation only occurs when they are
grossly intoxicated or drinking heavily. [Retarded] ejaculation is a relatively *rare* [my italics] variety of sexual dysfunction in the case of alcoholics who have been totally abstinent
for several months or years. This clinical data clearly indicates that intoxication and heavy drinking inhibit the ability
to ejaculate."

Even having and maintaining an erection is affected by
the use of alcohol. Dr. LoPiccolo writes: "Alcohol is often
thought to increase sexual desire by decreasing a person's
inhibitions. In small amounts, alcohol does tend to relax
people, which may or may not make arousal easier. In larger
amounts, alcohol has a negative effect on sexual desire, and
frequently it can interfere with the male's ability to have or
maintain an erection."

LOOKING AT THE BASICS

Here you are in sobriety, somewhat afraid to make a move
sexually because the failure fear has you in its grasp. You
need to take a serious look at the basic problems, because
before you can enter into successful solutions to these problems, you have to know all the elements that caused them.
For you it may have been:

Your very first sexual experience was a total failure.

You were laughed at, made fun of, or otherwise teased.

You were caught in the act of sexual experimentation.

A sibling, other relative, or friend "ruined" her life by getting pregnant and "having" to get married.

You found that by not having an ejaculation you were getting to be "quite a stud" because of your ability to endure.

You discovered that it wasn't really important for you to ejaculate to enjoy sex; you become anhedonic, i.e., not caring for or about your own pleasure.

This is a very short list. If you are in therapy, you will no doubt have the opportunity to find any other factors that might have been deeply buried, and been the source of your failure fear.

You have been using the drugs to either temporarily enhance sexual feelings or to overcome inhibitions that have prevented you from certain sexual activities.

Regardless of why you have used alcohol and other drugs, the key is to face the problem squarely, identifying what the problem is and then working on alternative solutions. For example, your guilt around religious beliefs and practices can certainly be helped by a visit or two to your spiritual adviser. If you don't have one, I suggest you *find* one.

If you don't find one of your faith, that's okay. I have found that most ordained men and women, expertly trained laity, and counselors can help put your fears to rest about the guilt issues that may have become such a part of your life.

Individual therapy can also be effective. I certainly recommend marital therapy where both you and your partner are able to work on guilt and performance issues with the help of a trained therapist.

THE IMPACT OF OTHER DRUGS

Alcohol, of course, isn't the only culprit. There are other drugs that by their use contribute to sexual dysfunction. The

August 5, 1983, issue of *The Medical Letter* states: "Many commonly used drugs can interfere with sexual function in both men and women, causing loss of libido, interfering with erection or ejaculation in men, and delaying or preventing orgasm in women. Drug-related effects on sexual function may be difficult to distinguish from the effects of depression or disease. . . ."

High dosages of some of the "most popular" and "in" drugs, those drugs that are central nervous system depressants, can wreck havoc on your sex life. These include alcohol, marijuana, heroin, methadone, antianxiety drugs, and many sedatives, all of which can cause low libido (desire), impaired erection, and delayed or no ejaculation in men, and no orgasm in women.

SUCCESSFUL FOREPLAY

When you fail to have successful foreplay, you are failing to enjoy one of the most beautiful and satisfying parts of human sexuality. And yet, if you are now in sobriety, the idea of engaging in long and artful foreplay may be very difficult for you. In the drinking mode, you may have been able to forestall actual orgasm because your central nervous system was depressed by the alcohol, thus enabling you to "do sex" for a longer period before culminating in ejaculation and orgasm.

But once again, here you are, wanting to just "get the thing over with" because you are sure that it won't be enjoyable or that you can't contribute very much to romantic foreplay. Without that glass or two of wine, that hit or two from a "joint," that line of coke, you have decided you are probably not the lover you were and therefore you don't wish to embarrass yourself or your partner by getting into long foreplay.

So you avoid it, and you also deny your partner the enjoyment of foreplay. You are missing so much of what the sexual experience can be. You see, for the first time, you have the opportunity to really *feel* things. What a joy it is to engage in the sensuous stroking of your partner's back or legs, arms, neck, and feet.

The art of erotic massage, the art of sensual massage are all possible now in sobriety, even if it remains as foreplay and doesn't culminate in sex. At first glance you might think that just engaging in sensuous foreplay and not moving on to intercourse or oral gratification is a completely frustrating waste of time. Not so.

THE BEAUTY OF FOREPLAY

Just think of spending literally *hours* with your partner, giving each other warm oil rubs, exploring with gentle hands and lips the absolute uniqueness of your partner's body! All of these are things you couldn't or probably didn't do in your alcohol/drug consumption days. Why? Well, first of all, if you tried lengthy foreplay the chances are you were going to fail because as you tried to extend the foreplay, you also drank or used more drugs, and soon you were unable to be very romantic, successful, or loving to your partner! You might have lost all interest in everything but your drug of choice.

But now there is an opportunity to explore the human body, to wander like a discoverer among the peaks and valleys of the person with whom you have chosen to share this most intimate of human experiences. And yet the failure fear has taken over. You may honestly believe that you are incapable of providing successful foreplay; you are sure that you will orgasm immediately, or that you will be clumsy, awkward, and laughable in your attempts.

There can really be no failure in foreplay if you stop to think about it. It either provides no pleasure, some pleasure, or a whole firecracker's worth! But in any of those cases, there is no failure, only degrees of success. It's all in the way you look at it, the manner in which you perceive the art of touching and feeling that can elicit such wonderful sensations for you and your partner.

How can there be such a thing as "failing" to discover? Discovering the way in which your partner feels when you have applied soft, warm oil, and gently massaged their entire leg (only) from the tip of their big toe to the outer edge of their hip?

Is this foreplay? You bet it is! Notice I described touching only your partner's leg and not the grabbing, routing, clutching motions of genital discovery that could very well have marked the only foreplay in which you previously engaged. What I'm driving at here is the willingness on your part to *explore*, with languid and time-consuming patience, the miracle of the person with whom you are sexually involved.

The art of sensory touching, which I believe to be the basic foundation of exciting, rewarding, and beautiful foreplay, is best found in Dr. Irene Kassorla's book *Nice Girl's Do*. I use this book for many of the couples I see in therapy; it's something like Dr. Alex Comfort's *The Joy of Sex* and *More Joy of Sex*, which couples can read and explore together.

When you think of foreplay, think of it as the acting out of your fantasies and dream passions; a prelude to the satisfying rewards of orgasm and ejaculation that await you if the acts are culminated in that fashion.

Dr. Seymour Fisher, a psychology professor and member of the National Institute of Mental Health, wrote a monumental work, *The Female Orgasm*, which studied three hundred middle-class wives who had volunteered to take part in this five-year piece of research.

In it, one finds case after case of foreplay description as varied and imaginative as possible: "One woman preferred not to begin the usual foreplay until her feet had been tickled for about ten minutes by her husband. Another enjoyed the sensation of air blown in her ear as part of the foreplay. . . .

Some women attained orgasm one or more times during foreplay. . . ."

Now how can one argue with the merits of foreplay and worry about failure fear when there is so much to discover? All this worrying seems like such a waste of effort when there are so many rewards at the end of the foreplay rainbow.

In short, you deserve to reap the benefits of enjoyable, prolonged, mutually satisfying foreplay. Techniques abound in many, many books. Videotapes, audio cassettes, even popular magazines address themselves to the many ways that you and your partner can experience the joys of sensual experiences that alcohol and other drugs have kept from you.

There is a veritable wealth of exploration in foreplay that will drive the notion of "failure" from your mind the more you practice and take the risks of making changes from alcoholic fumbling to skillful lovemaking.

So take heart. What at first seemed to be impossible goals are really achievable after all. You do not need alcohol or other drugs to be the "white knight" who will rescue you from fear and anxiety about sober sex.

No matter what the failure fear may be, there is a method, a way, a system that can help you overcome that fear!

Five

Am I Expecting Too Much?

It is not uncommon to think that once you have entered recovery, everything is going to be different; not only different, but spectacular. That simply isn't the case and the more you experience your sobriety and the more you live your life drug- and alcohol-free, the more you are aware that you are still going to have problems in your life, only now you will be in a position to face them and deal with them.

BEING REALISTIC

When setting goals, it is necessary to look for those that can be accomplished. So many people I have worked with over the years want to run right out and conquer whole new worlds of activity when all they really could accomplish would be to just play a *little* tennis, or ride a bike for a couple of miles. I use sports as an example because almost everyone can relate to the anxiety people feel when they think they are going to be tested every time someone suggests some sort of physical activity.

I always remember the man who wanted to do some "simple" climbing for recreation. Of course, he wanted his wife to join him. Unfortunately, she was afraid of heights, and she would have been a basket case doing what he had planned. He could not change his goal: to climb one of Colorado's beautiful mountain trails—and to do it in record time. The result was a rather prolonged and bitter fight because she refused to do more than a couple of hours' worth of hiking; he ended up on a ten-hour excursion and for the life of him couldn't understand why she was angry.

Setting realistic and accomplishable goals for sexual relations is equally important and necessary if you are going to gain much from exploring your new sobriety and sexuality. It is much better to set a goal that you have some certainty of reaching than to always be singing the "Impossible Dream," knowing that almost every goal you have set for yourself is impossible to reach and therefore will only add to your sense of frustration and low self-esteem.

Far better that you look at what can be new and different for you and what will make sense as you try and reorganize your sexual attitudes and goals. You may question the reason for having to set goals in sex at all; what's wrong with "just letting it happen"? Nothing. The problem arises because most people who are venturing forth in their new sober sexuality couldn't just let it happen when they were drinking or using; they *orchestrated* sex. In sobriety, it will be even harder to be casual around your sexual needs. The alcohol and drugs are no longer there to bolster your self-confidence, and so you have to have a plan or two for sex to work for you.

WHAT ARE UNREALISTIC EXPECTATIONS?

Before you can set about making a plan, it is essential to understand realistically what can happen and what is just plain out of the question. Some unrealistic expectations are:

Every person I meet is going to want to have sex.

I probably won't have any performance problems now that I'm sober and clean.

Now that I'm sober, I probably can have sex more frequently than before.

Sex is going to be terrific.

I am going to be an ideal sex partner now.

My interest in having sex is going to be greater.

MAKING A PLAN

Don't think that we're getting too technical here when I recommend that you make a plan for sex. Sex is no different than any other emotional or physical activity that requires your undivided attention, and there's the key. In sobriety, your senses are more keenly attuned. You will *feel* and you will *think* and not just *act* as you may have in the past. Thus, a *plan* is required; one that is easy to follow and has a reasonable chance of working.

People are often disappointed in some phase of their relationships because they have expectations; the problem is, they rarely share those expectations with their partner. So it becomes an automatic setup for failure.

REALISTIC EXPECTATIONS

There is much more to sex than the very act itself—that should be nothing new to you—yet it's so easily forgotten. In her book *For Yourself: The Fulfillment of Female Sexuality*, Dr. Lonnie Garfield Barbach says: "Although sex is one important aspect, much more than sex is involved in a loving relationship. Learning to be open, to share, to communicate, and be intimate in non-sexual ways also takes learning and practice."

The very heart of the sexual responses between two lovers is the relationship; thus it is necessary to build a *sober* relationship. Just about every response that you felt or every response that you were able to make your partner feel, is different now because the alcohol and the drugs are gone.

I have had many people challenge that statement, insisting that things were not different. But on close examination, most of the skeptics end up admitting that their sex lives *have* changed, whether for the better or for the worse.

All things hinge on the quality of the relationship, and that's why good communication, as well as the desire to share more than just your body with your sex partner, is important.

Every person I have worked with in treatment will tell me that he or she has expectations of what their relationship should be. When I press them on the question of whether they have ever shared these expectations with their partner, more often than not they've said no.

The reason most people tend to form expectations, to make very concrete plans about how they want their relationship to develop and grow yet never take that time to see if their partner might have the same expectations, is fear.

CREATING A "GAME PLAN"
People will formulate what seems to them to be a very playable "game plan," but may never have the talent to execute it.

Rather than risk losing the relationship, they keep their "game plan" to themselves and fear comes out the winner. When your partner fails to play, when he or she fails to live up to the expectations of your fantasy relationship, you become depressed, disappointed, and determined to change him or her!

This simply isn't going to work. What will work is talking openly, honestly, and in a spirit of mutual awareness about what you expect from your relationship *and* what you expect to give. All too often I hear couples in a session talk about how "all the changes that she wants me to make, but what about the ones I want *her* to make?" In other words, the partners in a relationship are often very anxious to have changes made by the other person in order to fulfill their list of expectations, but they are not as willing to make any changes to fit their partner's bill of particulars for a successful relationship.

When this happens I send the couple home and instruct them to make a list of their expectations. I ask them to head their list "What I Expect From a Relationship," and not to share the list with their partner until we are all together again in my office. When I compare the lists they are amazingly alike, but also dramatically different. The fact that the couple has been very secretive about their expectations is obvious when one sees the differences.

I recall a couple who was dating pretty extensively, but then began to run into trouble because she was really hitting the booze on certain occasions. They came to the Gateway Treatment Center to get help for her drinking problem. They entered treatment with us and she did very well, gaining her sobriety and generally improving the quality of the relationship.

When we started this couple on the couple's therapy part of the program, I asked them for the "Expectation List." The first two sessions with me they had forgotten to do their homework. The third time, she brought her list but he had "forgotten" his.

Finally, I collected the lists. Hers was carefully written on a yellow legal pad. His was scrawled on the back of an envelope, and I had a sense that he might have done it out in the parking lot before coming in for our session. Nevertheless, I took and compared both of them. She had some key "buzz" words heading her list: honesty, trusting, fidelity, and so on. Her partner had "camping and fishing" on his list as a high priority for what he wanted from her.

"Interesting," I said. "Terry has 'camping and fishing' pretty near the top of his list. How do you feel about that,

Meg?" Well, it turned out Meg really hated that sort of thing; her idea of "roughing it" was to have only a black-and-white TV in the Howard Johnson's motel room.

"But," Terry protested, "you always said you wanted to go! What the hell was that all about?"

"I didn't want to lose you, Terry," Meg replied, "but God, I hate that sort of thing! Why do you think I drank so much when we did that?"

Meg's alcohol problem was a lot more deep-seated than just an outdoor trip or two, but her attempts to always be a people pleaser were certainly contributing to her alcohol abuse. How much easier it would have been if Terry and Meg had spent a little time doing this kind of homework somewhere in their dating plans, if they could have "swapped" lists of expectations before their relationship became so involved that their arguments were escalating to full-scale fights.

Sharing expectations before you become locked into a relationship is not so different from knowing your prospective sexual partner's sex history. AIDS has prompted an entirely new way of approaching meeting, dating, having sex with, and cohabitating with someone else.

The big "pickup" line of the sixties and seventies, "What's your sign?" has been firmly replaced with, "What's your sexual history?" So what would make it so difficult to look at a list of expectations that you and your partner have for a relationship?

TESTING THE GOALS

I have two sets of three by five homemade index cards in my office that I use to test relationship goals. On the cards I have written individual words or statements, such as "Money," "Trust," "Loyalty," "Hugs and Kisses Without Sex," "Good in Bed," "Athletic Ability," and so forth.

The top card of each deck is marked, "What I Want in a Relationship." The rest of the cards are randomly placed in the deck, with no "stacking" on my part whatsoever. I then ask the couple to each take a deck and get down on the floor of my office in separate corners and begin to lay out the cards on the floor in their order of importance.

They must have the "What I Want in a Relationship" card on the top, but then they put the cards down in descending order of importance. I don't let them see what their partner is doing. When they are finished lining them up, I get them to sit in their chairs again and I pick up the cards and lay them out on the floor side by side, in the exact order that the patients had arranged them.

I asked the couple, "What do you see here?," and just let it all develop. They may have spent many sessions with me arguing about money and yet the "Money" card will be way down the list in both of their lineups.

We go through the lists lying there on the floor, seeing the differences in how they have been ranked in priority, and then I ask, "Is this list arranged with your current relationship in mind or is this what you want in *any* relationship?"

This generally is what I refer to as a "sleeper," because more times than not one or both of them will have let their fantasy list take over. They will have arranged their cards (like putting "Money" way down the line) the way they believe it should be, the way they fantasize a relationship to be, instead of how it really is with the person sitting with them in my office.

I then ask them how they would rearrange the cards with this particular person in mind. If both of them have said that the cards were arranged with only their current love partner in mind, then I ask them to arrange the cards in the order of their idea of just any relationship, clearly appealing to their opportunity to fantasize.

In this fashion, expectations can be looked at, examined critically, discarded or kept, talked over, built upon, changed, bargained over, and all the other things you can do when you are trying to hammer out a *workable* agreement between two people. So, this is a good point to look at just what a list of reasonable expectations could contain. I specifically say "could" instead of "should" because there are many variations that you will be able to offer that will be custom-tailored to fit your relationship.

THE FEMALE LIST

Starting from a woman's point of view I am most proud and happy to share my wife's list of her expectations in a relationship, a list that she made as an exercise for the research of this book. I have done no editing whatsoever, and the list was created by her in exactly the fashion that I have outlined for you. I simply asked her to write down her expectations of a relationship; I did not specify her "relationship with me."

MY STAND ON A RELATIONSHIP

1. I will be treated with love, respect, and compassion.
2. I will be loved for being exactly the way I am.
3. I will be acknowledged daily for my beauty, desirability, and commitment to improving myself and my life.
4. I will be considered successful.
5. What I have to say will be considered valuable.
6. I will be treated at all times as an equal partner in the relationship, contributing my skills, talents, and support to achieving whatever goals we set forth as a couple.
7. We will share a vision for our purpose as a couple.
8. Communications will be open, honest, direct, and kind. Items will not go unacknowledged. Communication will always be delivered in such a way that the relationship is empowered. We will be committed listeners.
9. I will be acknowledged daily as being special and important in my partner's life.

10. I will be compassionately supported in achieving my personal goals.

11. I will have frequent and regular sex with my partner as an expression of our love.

12. Whatever I say and do will be held in the context that I say and do it to nurture and support the relationship and each of us, out of my commitment to having the relationship work.

13. Our life together will be exciting and adventurous.

14. I will have a relationship that includes sexual exclusivity and fidelity, but that allows for friendships and time with friends and time alone for pursuing my own interests.

15. We will make a difference individually and as a couple.

16. We will enjoy and share abundance—in love, finances, success; in all areas of life.

Then she added a personal credo, based I think in some part on her understanding of what a nut I am on accepting personal responsibility; to wit: "I recognize that I am responsible for bringing forth this stand—and I will have someone in my life who shares this stand. I DESERVE IT."

What I particularly like about this list is the concentration on making sure that her own needs, particularly in the ego department, are met. She clearly believes that if she can't get support about feeling good about herself, and gain recognition for the accomplishments that she makes in her life, then she can hardly have much energy to put into a relationship.

I did not ask her to devise the list based on our relationship; I played it strictly by the same rules that I use with my patients. After she had handed me the list, I *then* asked her if she was thinking of our relationship or just any relationship. She quite honestly said that these were her personal goals for any relationship; however, she had no complaints that our relationship was not filling the list.

THE MALE LIST

Now for the men's list. This one is a compilation of several that my male patients have outlined for me over the years.

WHAT I VALUE IN A RELATIONSHIP

1. I will have a committed relationship, one my partner is willing to look at as having a future together.
2. I will have a relationship that is built on the ability to communicate with each other; the "silent treatment" will not be allowed.
3. There will be touching between us without the necessity of sex, but rather for the sheer joy of feeling one another's bodies.
4. I will expect that my partner will care about me, and allow me to care about her in all areas of her daily life.
5. I want to share my daily life with my partner and expect her to share with me on a feeling level, not just words.
6. I must be able to trust my partner and her fidelity to our relationship.
7. I will not share my partner sexually; if I do not meet her needs, we must talk about it and correct it together.
8. I want respect from her for what I do, for what I think.
9. I want her to be my friend; if possible, my *best* friend.
10. Our sex will be uninhibited and free from the constraints of past experiences. We will create our sexual passion together.
11. We will spend quality time together, and on a regular basis.
12. I want to share my fantasies and want her to share

her fantasies without fear or recrimination or guilt for having shared them.

This list from a man's standpoint has a little more emphasis on sexuality for the sake of sexuality than the woman's. However, it also features what I think is a good emphasis on the *quality* of a relationship. After all, if you don't have such things as honesty, fidelity, and a desire to share a life with a person, the rest will fall apart very quickly, I assure you.

The business of a man wanting someone who will "share her fantasies without fear" is a little tricky. Sometimes in the "heat of sexual passion" a man can convince his partner to "really let loose" and tell him her sexual fantasies; later, when the lovemaking is over, he makes her life miserable with recrimination. What was an answer to his request becomes a massive guilt trip for her for ever having bared her soul, and she is inclined not to do it again.

Recriminations can be avoided if this expectation list is shared early in the relationship, then the opportunity presents itself quite easily to accept or reject any or all of the expectations, and replace them with those that are mutually acceptable.

This may seem like a contradiction, but it isn't. Just like a contract, one does not expect that *all* of the terms, clauses, demands, and so on are going to be acceptable to the other party "out of hand." What the lists of expectations provide is a starting point, a sort of "springboard" to what will work for the two of you.

The most important thing to remember is that if you have some expectations going in to the relationship, and can openly share them by exchanging them, talking about them, and explaining exactly what you mean, then there is very little chance that something will come at you out of left field and wreck the relationship.

If you know what your partner's expectations are, then

you can at the very least discuss them, examine what the details of the expectations are, and then determine if they are something you can live with.

The idea is to devise the best possible way in which your needs can be met. But there aren't just your needs and your partner's needs to consider. You really have *three* elements that must be satisfied in a relationship. You want your needs met, you want your partner's needs met, and you want the needs of the relationship met. Your relationship is a living thing that needs attention and nurturing. When you begin to believe that the expectations on both lists are designed to make your relationship a solid and growing one, then it's easy to see how important it is that each of you meet or at least try to meet those expectations.

Breaking fidelity in your relationship, for example, will not only crush your partner, but it will also break a lot of the trust of the relationship. It will take the glow out of it and will make it suspect for continuing unless there is some very hard work to bring the luster back and pump new, fresh breath into it again.

THE FRAGILITY OF RELATIONSHIPS

A relationship is a fragile thing at best, particularly in the beginning. With sobriety entering the picture, the fragility returns because there is a mammoth doubting and questioning of whether you can maintain the intensity of a relationship *without* the alcohol. The sexual intensity that you seek in your expectations; the frequency and the quality of the lovemaking are all up for grabs; its' a brand new ball game. You can count on the fact that the relationship starts over as a living third party that will require much attention from both of you in order to survive and grow.

If you do the dishes together, that's helping to get a chore done; however, it's also nurturing the relationship because you can spend more quality time together. If, however, you are bitching every step of the way about "having to do chores," the relationship can wither and gasp for breath. When you really begin to help your relationship grow, you begin to think of all the little things you can do for each other and for yourselves, all the while realizing that the more you share with each other in the mundane things of daily living, the more you are able to share in the sensual and romantic part of your lives. The relationship breathes vigorously when it is being nurtured and treated with respect, with dignity, and, most of all, with *importance*.

Expectations can always be changed, altered, added to, or deleted altogether. It's a great deal of fun for couples to work on these expectations in the manner I have suggested. When you develop and discuss your expectations list, there may be points that you are not willing to give up — fidelity to this one partner, for example. You will not tolerate him or her fooling around sexually with someone else. Make sure that each of these points on your list are known as being "nonnegotiable," so there aren't bitter fights or disillusionments about them later.

The points that can be modified or replaced by a different expectation are the ones that become your "bargaining chips." One woman's list said she would not tolerate a smoker. Well, the guy she was with *was* a smoker and would not give it up; he felt he had already made a great sacrifice by going into sobriety.

It seemed they wouldn't get beyond this conflict until he suggested that maybe he could not smoke in their house but confine his smoking to their patio. She agreed to this compromise, although she said her major concern was for their health and really wanted him to consider giving up smoking entirely.

"One project at a time," he countered, and they dropped it. They struck an agreement, used some "bargaining chips" in their expectations, and, for them, it worked.

Six

The Importance of Commitment

I'm often amazed that most of the singles I see in treatment are still single. To look at them and observe them they seem like perfect candidates for a relationship. But then, after a few minutes of conversation, it becomes painfully apparent that they are absolutely *terrified* of making a commitment to another person.

Even worse is the fact that they are unwilling to even explore the possibility of a committed relationship with someone, as if just talking about it would be more than they could handle. It would not be fair to make a blanket statement that all single people remain so because they fear commitment, but growing numbers, men in particular, are remaining single far longer than a few years ago.

When I listen to the complaints of available women—that is, women who are interested in some sort of relationship—they run to a common thread: "It's tougher than ever to get a man to not be afraid to make a commitment!"

THE IMPORTANCE OF COMMITMENT

If you were to list the many elements that we use to define the word *love,* if we make a list of the emotions that we generally attribute to "being in love" and enjoying one another in a "love relationship" (as opposed to a platonic one), then the word *commitment* would have to be near the top.

I place it in first position in my own list of the elements of love. Let's look at the whole list so you can see how they tie together. This list of twelve "elements of love" came from a workshop on sexuality that I attended many years ago. The task before us was to think of all the elements that would comprise the feeling, emotion, and state of love.

Once listed, we could arrange the words in the order of their importance to us, with one exception: The word *sex* was to be last on the list. The reason? Very simple, really. When a person is into alcohol and drugs, "sex" is the number one thing on the list; very little time, attention, or effort is applied to any of the other human emotions that comprise the feelings of love.

Therefore, in sobriety, the task is to put the act of sex in the last position and to concentrate on the other eleven elements that have so long been ignored.

THE TWELVE ELEMENTS OF LOVE

1. Commitment
2. Communication
3. Caring
4. Sharing
5. Trust
6. Touching
7. Understanding
8. Friendship
9. Respect
10. Togetherness
11. Kindness
12. Sex

The reason "commitment" is number one on my list is that it is far and away the most important element in a love and (sex) relationship. Many couples list communication as their number one problem, and certainly that can't be discounted. The ability to talk and to listen to one another; the desire to share instead of just mouth words and phrases, is the very essence of a successful relationship, so "communication" deserves to be high on the list, but "commitment" remains in the top position.

COMMITMENT AS CHANGE

When we talk of making changes in life, we are really asking a lot. Most people, particularly those who have been under the yoke of chemical addiction, rebel against the idea of making changes. However, in order to experience wellness, and certainly to begin to look at sexuality in the light of sobriety, change is necessary, and commitment is the essence of change.

When you were drinking or drugging you probably weren't very interested in much permanence. Relationships might have been long term, but that does not mean there was much commitment to it. When you enter sobriety, putting away the bottle is only the first step. Making the necessary *changes* in your life, doing things in a different way, with perhaps different people, means that you will be asking yourself and others to take risks.

Making a commitment to a relationship is taking a big risk. The word itself from the Latin *committo*, means "to make over in trust." So certainly when you make a commitment to another person you are beginning the changing process that says you will trust not only the person with whom you are going to be involved, but you will trust the process of the relationship as well.

Sex, which is part of the elemental stages of love, needs to be nurtured through *all* of the other eleven elements, with commitment ranking high enough to say to yourself, "I am willing to put the necessary energy into making the changes that will be necessary for me to get the fullest degree of fulfillment from a sober sexual engagement."

It is very frightening for a man or a woman to think about what the word *commitment* entails: making a pledge to be *together* and *work* on the relationship as a couple. As I have said before, when a couple spends more time trying to decide whether they are even going to *be* a couple—more time, energy, and effort than working on the relationship itself—then that couple is generally in serious trouble.

When you get right down to what keeps such a couple together, you unearth problems that revolve around commitment.

COMMITMENT EXCUSES

The excuses for being unable to make a commitment run the gamut from "I'm afraid I'll get hurt again" to "I want to wait and see if this thing [relationship] will work out or not."

The latter statement needs some examining. How in God's name can anyone measure in advance whether something as fragile as a relationship, something so in need of nurturing and careful consideration, can ever succeed if, at the start, one of the parties is afraid to commit to making it work?

You are putting the cart before the horse when you think like that. First, it is necessary to start believing that "I *can* make a commitment in sobriety." *Then* comes the hard work on the other eleven elements of the "Love List"—communication, caring, sharing, trusting, and so on, and finally sex—that will enhance the relationship and make it grow.

Look at it this way. If all the energy that goes into wondering whether you should be a couple was applied to *being* a couple, doing things couples do, then you would be much happier and fulfilled. It requires commitment on both your parts.

COMMITMENT TO SELF

It's entirely possible that you are afraid to think about commitment; you don't see it as part of your sober life at all.

There is a lot of fear involved with commitment. In the first place, you may be frightened about commitment because of your past experiences. But do you really want that to be an excuse for the rest of your life? If so, you had better be prepared to be an emotional cripple, because that's what you are setting yourself up to be.

You will never find the right person, never be able to practice some of the new and exciting steps in this book, because you will never feel safe. Commitment, after all, means safety. It means that you don't have to worry, wonder, and fret about whether your partner is going to be there in the morning because you have both made the pledge to accept your couple status and concentrate on cementing the strength of it by practicing and improving your sexual skills.

To help you find strength in commitment, I have created a little acronym around the word, something to carry around with you in the active part of your brain. Certain words are italicized so you can use them as the keys to reinforcing the idea of commitment.

> **C** • I *care* about this partner.
> **O** • I can be totally *open* with him/her.
> **M** • I can *make* this relationship work.
> **M** • I can *mold* this relationship.
> **I** • I feel the *intrigue* of our relationship.
> **T** • I feel *total* when we are together.
> **M** • I feel our *minds* blending.
> **E** • I feel *energy* when I'm with him/her.
> **N** • I feel *nonthreatened* by my partner.
> **T** • I feel *trust* from my partner.

COMMITMENT TO THE RELATIONSHIP

The key words in the list apply not only to commitment to a relationship, but they can also be considered game plan words, words that you can use over and over to remind you of what your commitment is and what it means to your relationship.

All of the techniques and tools and games and fun and learning about your sexual growth that I will be sharing with you in the upcoming chapters is not going to amount to a hill of beans without your commitment. And the commitment does not just apply to a partner either. I am speaking of your commitment to take risks and to try the things that I will be helping you to explore. If you start off and get bored and discouraged, or decided not to follow the game plan, then you *will* fail, and probably fail again and again.

The sexual techniques are not good if you haven't put your relationship in good working order. It's just like recovery. There's no use in talking about what your recovery program will be like when you are still taking a drink "now and then." You are just kidding yourself. It's the same with sex and sobriety. We already know what your sexual life was like when you were drinking; what you don't know is what it can be like in sobriety.

During the ongoing lecture series at our Gateway Treatment Center I give a lecture entitled "Sexuality and Drugs," highlighting how things are different for people sexually when they stop using alcohol and other drugs, and giving some of the techniques and practices discussed in this book. It's always such a pleasure when a patient or couple tells me in a session, after they have heard this lecture, that they tried one or two of the things I suggested, and how delighted they were with the results.

They always seem so surprised that any of these things work.

"Well," I say, "what do you think made them work?"

"I'm sober for one thing," he or she will say. "I actually remember doing (whatever) this time!" And then as sort of an afterthought, "and I feel comfortable doing this with (insert partner's name) because it's so *special!*"

"And what's making it special?" I ask.

"Because we work at it together. We have a *commitment* to each other."

They have realized that they can put so much more energy into their relationship, or into their sex life, because they are not using their energy trying to decide whether they should even be together. They have made a commitment and that's more than half the battle right there.

ACCEPT RESPONSIBILITY

There is also a responsibility to one another to try and make things work in your relationship. You owe it to each other, and it's an ongoing debt, a fun one, that you shouldn't mind paying. Just getting beyond the idea that the relationship you are in, married or no, is only temporary is a big step that all couples have to take. It's too easy to assume that this relationship will be like "all the rest." That kind of thinking can wreck this whole outline for increased and rewarding sexual enjoyment in sobriety.

You must make sure that *this* relationship, clean and sober, is going to be different because you have it within your power to make it different. It's already not the same because you are not the same. You no longer drink alcohol or use drugs, therefore the experiences that you have now are different; you have not had them before.

Commitment to the relationship also implies commitment to risk, making the changes and taking the chances that these things will work. I cannot tell you how many times people tell me that they have read and followed the instructions for something I suggested in *The Joy of Being Sober;* they say to me, somewhat astounded, "That really works!" I usually thank them for "trusting the process" and taking the risk to prove to themselves what I have urged them to experience for themselves.

MAKE COMMITMENT WORK

Use the idea of making a commitment to yourself and to a relationship work for you. You do that by saying, "I will try these things not just once but two or three times. I will make a *commitment* to explore these ideas fully and discard what doesn't work for me, but keep, expand, and practice the things that *do* work."

That's really all that's required. You need to be willing to look at how things in your sexual life can be different from what they used to be. If you are successful in ridding your mental closet of everything that didn't work for you sexually, and look at what might work as I will outline it for you, then you are on your way to enjoying the sex and sobriety that I know is available to anyone willing to take the risk.

Being committed both to yourself and to the relationship will help you decide about the things you like sexually, and also about the things you don't like or are just plain unable to make work.

COMMITMENT IS POWER

You have a powerful new tool working for you when you make the decision to commit to a relationship. You can quickly cross the border of indecision and get right into improving the status of your relationship in its new light of sobriety and sexuality.

Remember that all the old rules don't hold true anymore. The old fears about commitment don't have to be there now that you are alcohol- and/or drug-free, because most of those fears were caused by the use of alcohol or other drugs. You were really creating a great field of insecurity around yourself and your ability to make and keep a relationship.

All that has no validity now. You are a different person and ready to make a commitment to a partner and to a relationship, pledging yourself and your energies to give this the best effort you can. Since this is a new idea for you, you don't have to worry about making mistakes. If you make wrong choices you have the power to correct them; if you take certain risks and they can't work for you, you can discard them and try another course of action. But because you have risked commitment, you don't have to waste energy wondering if there's someone better for you than the one you're with, or wonder if you really *want* to be in this relationship.

By making this decision, your commitment can now power up and energize the elements that you have been afraid to tackle in your life while you were drinking or drugging.

You are free now to apply whatever energies you choose toward your sexuality, comfortable in the knowledge that they are enhanced by commitment. You are finally deciding to be a "major player" in the relationship, instead of just a bystander waiting for a "sure thing."

Making the new techniques in this book work will, in turn, nurture the relationship and make it grow and prosper, and this will reinforce your plan for a new life of sobriety. Being committed both to yourself and to your relationship is healthy, because it reinforces the idea that you are capable of making decisions with a clear mind, and you are willing to take that fearless foray into your own sensuality and sexual enjoyment and fulfillment.

Seven

Do I Know You?

Sobriety produces not just a change in you the drinker, it also produces changes in the person you are with, giving that person new ways of treating you, of treating the relationship, and of acting and reacting to someone who is no longer drinking.

If both of you are in recovery then there are *two* new people in this relationship. The way you conducted your sex life when you were drinking or drugging, and the way your sexual partner responded to you, are totally different from the way you will act now and the way your partner will respond.

A CHANGED RELATIONSHIP

Your relationship has definitely changed. Some of the changes may be common to all couples, as well as to singles. I couldn't possibly know everything that has changed for you, but I can tell you two things that are very definite: (1) Whatever worked for your sexually in the past, may possibly *not* work now. (2) *Both* of you have changed, not just the recovering partner.

This second point also applies to singles. No matter who you may want to have a sexual relationship with, you are going to find that he or she has made changes to compensate for the new behaviors you are exhibiting. If you are the "significant other" in the relationship, you have changed just as much as the recovering person because you are no longer dealing with a person who is drinking or drugging. Neither their actions nor their reactions are the same as they were, and neither are *your* actions or reactions. You are a different person by the very fact that the game plan of your relationship has changed with the removal of the alcohol or the drug.

It's very important for you to realize that you need to keep an open mind. The way in which you handled a particular situation with your partner when he or she was actively drinking probably isn't appropriate now. What I like couples to do is just start off with some basics by performing the following little exercise in dialogue:

"Too much water has run under the bridge."

"Okay, let's give ourselves that" (and ask,)

"What would it take to build a *new* bridge where there hasn't been any of that old water?" (and then,)

"Could we build this new bridge one step at a time, with new or forgotten 'planks' that were once in our relationship?" (and finally)

"What do we do to get started?"

Remember: I am trying to get you to believe that you have to repair the *basic* relationship before the full impact on the *sexual* relationship can happen, so don't think these exercises are just a waste of time. I assure you, they are not. Further, these same exercises apply whether you are part of a couple or a single. The problems remain the same.

Let's break the questions down and look at them in more detail.

TOO MUCH WATER HAS RUN UNDER
THE BRIDGE

Well, sure it has. And ultimately that's what all relationships discover. With the ebb and flow of the lives of any two people living together or even just mutually committed to a relationship, there are daily, and even hourly, changes. People get different jobs, look at different locales in which to work and live, take on more or get rid of different responsibilities. All of what we can simply call "life problems" affect every relationship, and if you consider that your life is an ever-flowing stream from its start until its end, then it's natural to assume that lots of life's water has run under your bridge!

However, when this expression has been used in your life, it's mostly been in a negative manner, hasn't it?

"Boy, a lot of water has sure run under the bridge!"

"Oh, well, I just don't care; it's water under the bridge!"

"Can't we just let it be water under the bridge, for God's sake?"

In each of these exclamations we see a negative connotation, a fact of life that we just have to accept now because it's already gone, passed under the bridge of our lives. And in the context that so much of that expression really speaks to the negative part of our relationships, then it ought to be okay to just let go of it, and watch it pass under the bridge!

We can't go running downstream and block up the negative aspects in our lives that have already passed and make them right again. So what makes you keep hanging on to whatever negative influences have been in your life? You do it because they have become comfortable for you. Painful, maybe, but still comfortable. If there has been infidelity in your relationship, it's hopefully over now. What possible good can come of constantly resurrecting the affair and rehashing what you two have been over time and time again? Better to allow that episode to be "water under the bridge."

I am not asking you to whitewash the pains that have happened in your relationship, but rather I am asking you to consider if there is any real payoff for you in keeping them dammed up under your life's bridge? I think not. Unblock the twigs, sticks, and stones that you have employed and let the hurtful past truly be "water under the bridge," once seen, used, and now ready to be discarded forever!

In a more positive vein, both of you can agree that in the past each has contributed to hurting the relationship. Both of you made mistakes, mistakes that you often tried to fix with sex. Remember the times you spend hours in a bitter fight only to have the fight "'resolved" by hitting the sack? That's a pretty unsatisfactory way to deal with the problems in a relationship.

Without having to throw darts at your partner, without having to point any more fingers and drag out all the heavy weapons in your arsenal, let's just agree to let it all go, and let the waters go ahead and flow as muddied as they may be under your bridge and out of your life. What we are looking for is the possibility that as long as that old bridge (relationship as it was) remains, it may not be possible to ever get clear, untroubled water flowing under it. Maybe it will never be secure enough to support the weight of these two new people who are seeking to cross that brown, ugly water of the past. The old bridge may not be adequate, so you'll need to build a new one.

BUILDING A NEW BRIDGE

Like any other building project, building this new bridge can be overwhelming when you try and absorb the whole thing at once. I have vivid memories of the first house I ever built from scratch. When I think of the enormity of the project it still scares me. It was impossible to cope with all that I had to learn in order to build that house, but you know, taking one little piece at a time, it became possible. I needed a lot of professional help to guide me, but nevertheless it was *possible!*

Even today, when I am in my workshop examining a

complicated piece of furniture that I want to build for some-one's Christmas present, it just plain overwhelms me. But then I begin to look at just how to do little details, how to set up jigs to make all the drawers at once, or how I can organize my "production run" between routers, saws, and drill presses so that I can take a piece of raw wood from rough dimen-sions through to a finished piece that hopefully fits right in just as it was planned.

It's exactly the same with your new relationship bridge. You build it one plank at a time, with the objective being to build it as a brand-new project. You may make mistakes, but they will be identified and fixed.

I have identified some basic "planks" that seem to fit all couples in recovery. If you are single, these planks still ap-ply. You don't have to be in a committed relationship to have the need for a new bridge to help you cross into a life of sober sexual fulfillment.

THE SEVEN PLANKS

1. Dating renewal and the "blind date."
2. Old tape replacement.
3. Trust deposits and withdrawals.
4. Forgetting as well as forgiving.
5. No TV meals.
6. Spiritual renewal.
7. Sharing chores.

You may look at these seven items and wonder how they can affect your sexual relationship, but I am asking you to trust the process, and remember that *any* bridge stands be-cause of the soundness of its planks.

These planks give you a safe, firm passage from a dys-functionate sexual relationship to a rewarding, fulfilling, and sharing one. They will also improve the overall quality of your relationship.

The new bridge is basically unencumbered with the muddy waters of the past, when alcohol and/or drugs were involved. Once you have built the new bridge, you will be ready to cross to the other side and the "new" other person in your life and to expore your sober sexuality.

A word of caution: Don't get stuck on the specifics of what is wrong in your relationship. Concentrate on what *can be* and that helps us look upward and not down and back.

Always try to work on these planks without becoming distracted by thoughts of "this won't work!" or "I've tried that." Just trust the process of building.

Once you have developed and practiced these seven planks, you may want to add some that are uniquely your own. Remember, however, that these are the basics and should be firmly in place before adding more.

Okay, with those simple ground rules, let's tackle these planks one at a time and see if they make sense to you and whether you can use them in the new bridge in your life. If you or your partner thinks this is a "silly" exercise, or "not worth anything," then you are doomed to stay in the dysfunctional stage that now exists. You have to be willing to take action to make changes, and changes require work and a desire to make things different.

First Plank: Dating Renewal

Be honest. When was the last time you and your partner had a date? I'm talking about a genuine preplanned event. It has kind of slipped into the habits of the past, hasn't it? After all, you have each other, so what is the purpose of dating?

That's the very reason for making this a plank in the first place. You have taken each other for granted. If you are single, then you have assumed that you can always get a date if you want one. (You didn't have any trouble before, did you? As long as you could buy a drink or a line, you always seemed to have a date.)

If you are a couple, the two of you need to be setting

some priorities in the relationship. If you are single, taking care of yourself on a social basis has to have priority. I want you to be making something *special* out of being together, even when the possibility of a sexual encounter doesn't exist. Couples: I want you to get fired up about just being together, making plans on a regular basis to be out, alone, and paying attention to each other. Singles: I want you to do the same thing; namely, planning on going out and getting back into the dating picture—without drinking or drugging this time—and doing it.

The couples I work with must agree to have a real date once a week. It doesn't matter what day of the week they pick. With today's hectic schedules, equal work responsibilities between partners, and day care, sitter, and money pressures, *any* day will work, just so it's weekly.

Having the date means taking the responsibility for all details of the date. It doesn't start and stop with "Wanna do something Friday night?" It starts with whoever is making the date *taking all* the responsibility for it. If, for example, the man is going to ask his partner for a date, and if there are children involved in the relationship, then I expect him to arrange all the "sitter details." That's part of the dating game as far as this plank is concerned. It is also mandatory that whoever is asking for the date have a specific event in mind.

If you have a partner, he or she needs to be putting enough effort into this thing to make you (and ultimately him or her) feel really special. If you are single, I want you to have the same sense of purpose. You are going out as a treat for yourself, something special, so it's important that you put some effort into the planning and details. You may not think this is necessary, but it is.

Whoever is planning the date can say whether it's for a movie, or dinner, or both; a concert, a play, or what have you. For example, if it is a dinner and movie date, then I want the initiator to have a specific movie and a specific restaurant in mind. If you are going alone, you still need to have a specific set of objectives for the evening. If you don't like the movie or the restaurant suggested by your partner, then you can counter with suggestions of your own.

For couples, it doesn't really matter what activity the date is built around. What's important is setting a specific time that the two of you can spend in conversation and togetherness. There may be a problem. Communications between the two of you may be so snarled now that sobriety has seemingly tightened up the tongues that you actually fear sitting across the table from one another in a public place. Many couples tell me that they dread the silences these meals cause, so they buffer themselves by always having other people around. A possible solution to these silent dinners is going out to eat after the movie, and using the movie as a point of conversation. Singles can use either the dinner or the movie as a conversation starting point when trying to meet someone new instead of the old "Can I buy you a drink?" ploy.

Some of the singles and one of my couples discounted this idea until I got them to agree to try it. The singles said they felt comfortable without the booze for the first time; their confidence in their ability to make small talk was restored. The couple reported being "utterly amazed" at how much they had finally *talked* to each other; talk that had been blocked for all the weeks that he had been in recovery. What did they talk about? Their kids? No. Her career? No. His struggling business and its resultant pressures? No. They talk for *hours* about the dumb movie!

However, once they had exhausted the pluses and minuses of the film, this couple swung quite naturally into some of the problems that were surfacing in their relationship. They are maintaining a once-a-week dating schedule, and guess what? Their sex life is improving, too. She reports that she feels "much closer" to him than before because he has "interesting things to say" to her, something that she had forgotten in all the years of his drinking and even from when they first got together back in college.

My singles report finding it easier to be "themselves" and

are becoming better listeners than before. They are also increasing the frequency with which they are being asked for second and third dates.

These weekly dates are not preludes to a wild night of sex, although it might end up that way. You should plan the date for its own sake, a way to simply share the experience of being with your partner and with no thought of a physical payoff. That would totally defeat the purpose of this new plank in your bridge because it resembles too closely your old *drinking* behavior, when sex was the culmination of both the date and the drinking. So go out on the date just for its own sake, to get to know your partner again.

Do you have to spend a lot of money? Absolutely not. What's wrong with a simple picnic for two? Of course, I expect that whoever made the date will also have made the picnic and done the planning. That's special! How about just a walk holding hands? Or a bike ride? The family dog would certainly welcome a regular time when the two of you spend thirty minutes or an hour just walking together, hand in hand on a beautiful morning or evening. Maybe you end up getting a yogurt or ice cream cone together. That's okay. Remember a "date" just needs to be a planned event that gets the two of you to spend some time together—some *quality* time.

The "blind date" is even more fun. Once a month, or at least once every three months, I want you to have a "blind date." Here's how it works. Whoever has drawn the assignment of planning the date (I use a coin flip) tells the partner only what he or she needs to know to prepare for the date. For example, "You'll need a light jacket, dress shoes, kind of dressy clothes," or maybe, "You'll need a bathing suit, but also pack an overnight bag."

The destination or plan for the "blind date" is disclosed only after you are under way. It may sound really dumb, stupid, or juvenile, but I assure you, it's *fun*. Let me give you an example. Several years ago I was seeing a young couple whose sex life was a shambles ever since he started recovery.

He felt awkward, unyielding, unskilled in lovemaking, and generally ugly (he was not). She sensed that he found her unattractive (she was not) and was building walls. The two of them were "constantly" bickering. He had become jealous of the fact that while he was "just a carpenter," she was a legal secretary and constantly going to the office "dressed to kill." She also began going to a local bar for drinks with her fellow office workers, including some of the attorneys. He became jealous and unable to see any payoff to his months of sobriety. He was thinking that "maybe I should start drinking again so she'll want me!" That's pretty self-destructive and relationship-destructive. In therapy, we started using, among other things, the dating plank for a new relationship bridge. It went extraordinarily well for several weeks, and then came time for the "blind date." The carpenter outdid himself and gets the award for the best acting job in many a season of my using this technique.

Taking great risks to himself and his natural shyness (in sobriety) and his low self-esteem, he went, without her knowledge, to the head of the law firm for which she worked. He told the boss about the couple's therapy and asked for cooperation on their "blind date" project. He got cooperation and *then* some! Our carpenter friend had made arrangements to spend the weekend at a wonderful hotel in the Colorado mountains. He got his folks to take care of their two children for the weekend. Just before noon on a Friday afternoon, he burst into the law office demanding to see his wife.

The whole office was in on the scam, of course, and they pretended to be quite upset at the ruckus this guy was making, raising hell about her "needing to come with him, right now!" She was mortified, to put it mildly. But the husband, suddenly confronted by her "irate" boss, said he was "kidnapping her" and she "wouldn't be back until Monday!"

At that, this strapping guy swept his wife up in his arms and carried her out of the office, with her fellow workers cheering loudly and yelling "Have a great time!" and other encouraging remarks. The wife, now on to the game, was wonderfully surprised and pleased as they went off for a great weekend of fun, frolic, and lovemaking, intermingled with the first good conversation and problem-solving days they had enjoyed in some time.

Was this a complex plan? Not really, but it *did* take planning and work on his part, and as I said earlier, a lot of risk in involving her office. But this man wanted his relationship and he also wanted his sobriety to continue and grow. The work of getting the "blind date" plank into place in their bridge to a new relationship paid off exquisitely. He had even packed her suitcase with everything she would need for the weekend in the Rockies. His thoughtfulness and his originality, his *giving priority to* their relationship, dispelled her fears that it was all over between them, sexually or otherwise.

They continued over the remainder of their therapy with me to have their regular weekly date; her "blind date" for him was taking him to stock car races that he was gung-ho about and that she had steadfastly refused to attend. Her unselfishness and her giving priority to their relationship just helped things get better. They are still together. He is still sober. They recently sent me a Christmas card and all it said was, "Still Dating! Thanks!"

Some singles I work with got involved in a group at one of the churches in the area and began signing up to go with a group to special "dates" such as movies, concerts, and the theater. It became a special night out for these singles; something they looked forward to and made room for in their busy lives.

Second Plank: Old Tape Replacement

What is an "old tape" anyway? Earlier we talked about a person's "life script" being written when they are about four or five years old. You start getting "tapes" in your brain as to how you should react physically, psychologically, emotionally, and socially, to problems that come your way. In short, the real you is a person who makes and stores tapes in the brain's memory bank and then plays those tapes throughout life.

You have had good, even great tapes in your life; you have also had some real bummers—bad experiences, bad memories, bad things that have happened to you. Your drinking and drugging is a good example of a whole set of bad tapes that were put into the "tape deck" of your mind, ready for you to replay over and over in life.

This is one of those plank's that may be especially hard to add to your bridge; old tapes have been such an integral part of your life for so long that it will be hard to destroy them. But what we are going to do is look at the ways that you can replace those old tapes with new ones, ones that won't cause you pain, anxiety, anger, and finally, resentment.

Old tapes really get in the way of a relationship, preventing it from being healthy. And yet, as I said, they are so comfortable to play. What's the reason? Well, just like a favorite song, with old tapes you know how they start, where the middle section is, what the chorus is like, and finally how it ends. You could practically whistle the tune of an old emotional tape, you know it so well! So let's look at some new tools in the form of questions you can ask yourself:

1. When my partner does something to annoy me, does it trigger an old experience that happened with someone else?
2. An I unable to recognize an old tape when it starts playing?
3. Does the playing of that tape inevitably lead to an argument or a fight?
4. Do I ever confront my partner with the behavior that is causing my old tape to play?
5. Do I start using my "weapons" in defense of the old tape instead of admitting that it is playing?
6. When engaging in sex, do I have old tapes "shut me

down" as an expression of my anxiety or fear, instead of telling my partner what's really going on with me?

If you're like most people, the one exception would be question four where you probably answer "no." These questions are designed to show you two things: first, you are not alone, since most people answer the same way if they are being honest; and second, you can change the answers by changing the tapes. Question four becomes particularly vexing because it asks you to make a really big change; it asks you to think about not accepting your partner's behavior.

Verbalizing Old Tapes

When an old tape starts playing, *immediately* verbalize it to your partner. Tell him or her that what was just said or done started an old tape that you had with: (1) previous drinking or drugging behavior, or (2) a previous partner, whether a marriage partner or not.

This is a risky business, particularly the part where you may have to mention a person from your past, but it's necessary if you are to replace the old tape. You need to immediately recognize that things have changed. This isn't the old partner, nor is it the old circumstances where you or your current partner are numbing yourself out with alcohol or some other drugs.

Your partner's role in changing old tapes is to remind you that he or she isn't the other person. He or she also needs to ask you, "What did I say or do that started the old tape?" This should be followed by, "What can I do or say in the future that will make it okay for you?"

A very simple formula is at work here. The formula simply says that a behavior that is reinforced will cause repetition of that same behavior.

When your partner does something you don't like—perhaps something sexual, like performing oral sex on you— and you no longer have the alcohol to block your inhibitions but you say nothing about it to your partner, you are setting yourself up for a repeat performance. As a matter of fact, you may be afraid to damage your relationship by saying anything to your partner. Instead, you may pull an award-winning performance acting like you are enjoying it. The minute you do that you reinforce that this must be okay, so the next time, the behavior—in our example, oral sex—is repeated. You just lie there and suffer with the old tape in control!

You can count on the fact that every time you reinforce a particular behavior it will be repeated. You may not recognize an old tape when it is playing; you simply know that you are not comfortable with what is happening. This is where your partner can be helpful. If he or she can ask you if "there is an old tape playing," it might just get you to make the connection. Whatever you do, don't let the revealing of old tapes become destructive to your relationship! You need to reassure each other that the purpose of talking about an old tape is to replace it so it doesn't continue to cause barriers between you, damaging your relationship. You'll be amazed at how quickly you can replace an old tape with your partner's cooperation and with the sincere desire on both your parts to make the change.

For example, in the situation where oral sex causes discomfort, it can be played out from the beginning if you will acknowledge that this has always been a problem for you and that the alcohol simply masked the problem. You and your partner can then ask what it is about oral sex that makes it difficult for you, and then what *both* of you need to do to overcome that anxiety.

Perhaps one of the unspoken anxieties will be that you fear you will have to break your sobriety if you're ever to have oral sex again. If this is a particularly important issue for your partner (having oral sex), then it will be absolutely necessary that you talk about the anxiety to help prevent a relapse. You can count on your old tape playing everytime unless you have verbalized the fear and found a way to replace the old tape with one that says, "This is good. This is not harmful to me. This is an act of love between us, and it is natural." And most important, "I do not have to return to drink to enjoy or even participate in this."

Practice replacing the old tapes of your relationship by writing down the tapes that seem to be playing the most and then writing down the destructive behavior they cause. Talk, talk, talk to your partner about these old tapes and together take them out of your collection, replacing them with new, reinforcing behaviors that work to strengthen the relationship.

Third Plank: Trust Deposits

Trust is so important to the rebuilding of a relationship that it should be a plank that you take extra care and time installing so that you really understand it. Let's define what I mean by the term *trust deposits*.

Almost every partner in a relationship wants to assume control of the relationship at one time or another. When trouble occurs, such as an affair, whether it be a one-nighter or a long-term relationship, trust is put to the test. Over and over a partner will sit in my office and say that the number one problem in their relationship is "whether I can trust him/her again!"

This is really an attempt by one partner to take control of the trust issue when the issue is really with the other partner. The offending partner is the one who clearly has to deal with making what I call "trust deposits" in the bank of your relationship.

Placing the Trust Where It Belongs

I ask the partner who is struggling with trust to write the word *trust* on a piece of paper. When this is done, I ask that person to pass the paper over to his/her partner.

"You are giving the 'Trust' to him," I will say, "and it is strictly *his* responsibility to deposit that trust in the bank of your relationship." I go on to explain that she is no longer responsible; she has given over the control of the trust to her partner who broke it (the trust) in the first place. Then I ask,

"What is the consequence if he (or she) does this again?"

The aggrieved person then states his or her consequence, such as, "If he has another affair I will leave him!" or, "If she continues to raid our savings account without discussing it with me, I will close it, or have her name removed from it!"

Once the consequence has been stated I make sure the other party understands it, and that it *will* happen if the trust is broken by a repetition of the offending behavior.

"Now put the word *trust* in your billfold (or purse) and carry it with you," I will say. "You have just had the first deposit made for you by your partner. When you continue to nurture the relationship and not repeat those past behaviors, you are building up the balance in your 'trust deposit' account."

The couple also hears, "If you screw up and repeat that behavior, not only will you have depleted your 'trust deposit,' but you may have run it down too far and she (or he) will carry out the consequence as stated."

This is a good way to help the "controlling" person understand that the matter of trust doesn't belong to her/him at all, but instead rests with the person who broke the trust in the first place. It's very effective, and if you just "trust" this tool, you will see a great difference in your relationship bridge.

I have had couples whose sexual dysfunction began to clear up after they started work on this "trust deposit" idea. The letting go of responsibility for trust of the other person was the block that was removed in their sexual problem, as well as in their entire relationship. Always being in a care-taker role often leaves no time or space to be the partner you really want to be. Give up that tiresome and worrisome role and you will gain new energy for your relationship.

It isn't always going to be as easy as just using the "trust bank" idea. You're going to have to do some hard work to replace old tapes of no trust with new tapes of trust.

Verbalizing Trust

When you sense that trust is an issue between you and your partner, verbalize it. For example, say to him or her, "I have a feeling that you don't trust me when I tell you I'm just going to be with my friends." Then follow that statement with: "What do I need to do or say that will help you be okay with me and with my plans right now?"

Of course, the answer might come screaming back, "Don't go!" That's probably not acceptable to you, so keep pressing the point of what assurances your partner needs from you that will allow him or her to stop playing the old tape of no-trust that involves you.

What you are doing here is acting in a nondefensive way on the matter. You are attempting to gently put the ball back in your partner's court and asking him or her to give you a guideline of action or words that will help them be okay with your going out with your friends.

Now let's take the other side of the picture. Suppose it's you who is having a hard time with trust and are playing one of your old tapes. Again, verbalize your concern and your lack of trust. Say, "I'm sorry. I know this is an old tape, but I am having a really hard time with your going out with your friends this evening without me."

If your partner says something like, "That's *your* problem; you just don't trust *anytime* I'm out without you," don't get defensive and don't rise to the bait and go on the attack. Instead, acknowledge that it's your problem, just as you already said, and then ask if your partner could do or say something else that would help you to replace your old tape.

You might ask, "Could you call me when you get there?" Or, "It would be helpful if you would not stay out late."

Use your own words, of course, but the point is to verbalize your mistrust and offer some practical suggestions that your partner can employ to help you replace the old tape with a new one of trust about the event, people, places, or things that are causing you to have misgivings.

I want to reemphasize the point about your acknowledging that it is your trust, or rather lack of it, that is the issue there, and the thing that is causing the discomfort. That's the reason you are telling your partner about it and seeking ways that he or she can help you get rid of that old tape.

Anytime you can tie the missing trust into the past behavior of drinking or drugging that created the old tape in the first place, it's good. It's a double reinforcement first for your sobriety or staying clean, and second to realize that this *is* an old tape that needs replacing. If you don't replace it, it can damage the quality of the relationship; it could even break it up if you can't get past the trust issues.

Fourth Plank: Forgetting as Well as Forgiving

I know you've been dreading this plank. It's tough and not always successful, but at least we can explore its importance to your relationship and the impact on your sexuality.

How many times have you said, "I can forgive, but I just can't forget!" Or course some people like Queen Elizabeth I, had a hard time forgiving, as in the time she told the Countess of Nottingham, "God forgive you, but I never can." It's just plain tough to forget all the hurts, the wrongs, the punishment that humans inflict on one another.

I like what Bishop Henry King, who lived from 1592 to 1669, said about it:

We that did nothing study but the way
To love each other, with which thoughts the day
Rose with delight to us, and with them set,
Must learn the hateful art, how to forget.

Learning how to forget *is* hateful. You don't want to let go of that particular weapon, and yet it is so important to your relationship that you do. How can you possibly truly forgive if you do not forget the act that caused the pain? Easier said than done, but necessary.

A friend of mine, Dr. James G. Emerson, wrote in his book *The Dynamics of Forgiveness*, "That forgiveness was the basic quest [of the early church] can be documented if forgiveness is defined as that dynamic wherein one *becomes free to be a new creature*" (my italics). That's what your relationship goals should be: a relationship where forgiving has set you free, allowing you to be a new creature.

Forgiving is essentially an easy thing to do. One has only to promise "not to do it again," or better yet, "if I hadn't been drunk I wouldn't have done it." Somehow you then manage to find the strength to forgive. But as the days or years go by, you find yourself recalling the hurt, recalling the incident even though you thought you were done with it.

Time after time in sessions with patients I touched a nerve of a past, hurtful experience. Suddenly their eyes begin to fill with tears and the person who swore they were "over it" is reliving the experience. "God, I thought that was behind me!" is what they often say. The confrontation that the person has forgiven but not forgotten soon plays out with one or the other person demanding "When will you let me off the cross" and "What in God's name do I have to do so you forget that?"

Building the Future

When you discuss setting this plank in place you are already making a commitment to forget the past and build on the future. If you don't, there is little hope. You will continue to call on the hurt to justify the way you feel and give you more reasons to never grow and continue with your relationship.

I recall an incident when I was dining with a couple and she called her husband by her first spouse's name. At first there was laughter between them over the incident, but the remarks soon turned to scornful and hateful. The wife told me many months later that he could "never forget that I had called him by my first husband's name!"

Well, this guy didn't *want* to forget. He was using that as a means of blaming her over and over for his own impotence in bed. What was really causing his failure to be the sexual partner she wanted was his drinking, which got progressively worse. But he kept using that one incident as a weapon against her, all the while protesting that he had long ago "forgiven" her for still "having thoughts" about her ex-husband.

I have created a sort of pledge for couples that I now give to you, and charge you with taking it to heart; sort of the "nails" to this plank:

THE FORGIVENESS PLEDGE

I love you so much that not only do I forgive, but *together* let's let the incident be forgotten. I promise that I will not use it as a weapon against you. I will work my hardest to erase the incident from my memory, but if I slip, I will apologize to you and ask your forgiveness for bringing the pain back to your heart.

I ask you to help me forget by not teasing or tormenting me, even in anger, with any remembrances that might cause me to bring the incident back to my mind.

I pledge my efforts on our behalf, forgetting the past, forgiving the present, and exalting our future together.

If you are not ready to forget, then essentially you are not ready to forgive. The two fit hand-in-glove and to attempt one without the other just won't work. You will slip on this plank probably more than any other, but if you keep working at it you will soon learn the benefits of at least tying together the idea of both forgiving *and* forgetting.

Just remember that all the payoffs in this new bridge belong to both of you as a couple. As you strengthen the planks in the new bridge, the opportunity to increase the sexual experiences between you will present themselves more often and with clearer purpose.

One of the surest ways I know of for you to address the question of forgetting is to be open and honest with your partner. Tell him or her that you are having a very difficult time forgetting what has already been forgiven. The partner should then say: "What do I need to do or say that will help you forget?"

The purpose here is to get to your agenda. The other person can demand that you forget, can rave and rant that you "never want to forget no matter what I do!," but essentially he or she needs to find out what *you* need to have happen for the forgetting process to begin.

He or she could list a hundred things that should be done to make you forget, and none of them would hit the mark. Only you can say what is needed to help you forget and to let the healing start.

Practice forgiving and forgetting and *don't* discard it as being too difficult. Remember that the hurtful things may have been in your relationship for a long time, but you or your partner were using alcohol or some other drug to ignore them.

Now, in your sobriety, forgiving and forgetting become the soothing balm that will replace the alcohol. Not only can forgiving and forgetting be a solid plank in your new bridge, but it can be a direct line to more complete sexual abandonment, truer feelings, and more rewarding experiences that have been suppressed for a long time by the weapons of anger, fear, and revenge that keep you from forgetting.

Over and over again, patients tell me that they just can't get interested in sex because their "intimacy" or their "communication" with their partner is so poor; sobriety has only managed to underscore the fact that there were other problems to be solved besides the chemical dependency! Therefore, we shall continue to build our new relationship bridge and lay in the last three of the basic planks.

Fifth Plank: No TV Meals

Do you have any idea how many times you have had dinner with Walter Cronkite, Tom Brokaw, Peter Jennings, Connie Chung, or your local anchorpersons? Most of the time you and your partner have spent the dinner hour, or really the dinner twenty minutes, in front of the TV. Think about it. When was the last time you sat down, just the two of you, and enjoyed each other's company; asking questions about each other's day, getting answers to problems that you wanted to discuss?

If you are honest, it's been a long time. The television is a third-party buffer between you and your partner that you are perfectly willing to let do the communicating for you. I have nothing against television, but it is most often used to drive a wedge between two people. I know it is difficult for you to think of a meal without either the TV or your children. All I'm asking you to do is "trust the process," as I tell my patients, and try just one meal a week without *either* the kids or the television. Just think about the times when you were dating; you certainly didn't have every meal with kids (siblings or yours from a previous relationship) hanging over you, did you?

No, of course not. You found a way to have dinner, lunch, or breakfast alone. You probably didn't have the TV on either, since you were both out to charm and impress each other. Have *one* meal where the two of you are just sitting opposite each other and learning how to not only enjoy your food again but possibly begin to enjoy each other's company.

You can even make watching TV a new experience by selecting together the programs that you might want to see on a particular day or night. After all, when you were dating, didn't the two of you at least talk about what movie you might want to see? Or did you just let your partner lead you around by the ring in your nose?

Treat the TV watching as a date, be selective and have your meal(s) without the presence of "big brother" staring at you. When you get the hang of one meal a week, you can advance to two or three. Not all of your meals can be taken without other family members, but you will be amazed at the difference it makes to have the TV off when you eat!

Even kids and mothers-in-law will benefit by attempting conversation again, at least once a week for a start. Let's assume it is just the two of you now, and you have agreed *no TV* at this particular meal. Start by getting away from the dinner table to eat and try taking your meals at the coffee table or sitting on the floor with just candles to illuminate the scene.

This plank will help you get back the basics of your relationship, the romance and conversation that brought the two of you together in the first place. You have spent a long time allowing the TV to be your mealtime entertainment instead of looking to each other and the joy of just being together, uninterrupted by others. Without the TV you will find again the ability to talk to each other and, even more important, to listen to each other. A no-TV meal can be a wonderful prelude to an evening of romance, with all the trappings of the candles and perhaps some music playing unobtrusively in the background. The idea is to set the mood, and turning off the television is a big first step.

Sixth Plank: Spiritual Renewal

You may wonder how spiritual renewal fits into a book that is primarily dealing with sex, but I assure you it does. The whole act of sex, the very nature of two people sharing the mysteries and wonderment of their bodies, is a gift from life itself. The God of your understanding has made it possible for you to be sensual and sexual, has made it possible for you to experience untold beauty and warmth and the limitless feelings and expressions of joy and love and the sharing of one another.

When you were in the drinking or drugging state, sex was treated pretty selfishly. In sobriety, in being clean from drugs, you are starting over with finding that wonderment and beauty, that thrill and experiential sharing between two people. It will be different from what it was before, and one of the ways that you can savor what is sure to come is to renew some form of your spiritual lives.

Maybe the two of you had no spiritual life together before; if not, you should consider the possibility of putting some spiritual meaning into your lives together as a means of building a new relationship.

It doesn't matter if you go to "his" church or "her" church; it won't make a bit of difference if you don't go to church at all. What will make a real impact on your relationship will be the realization that your lives can be more complete and fulfilling if there is a spiritual bond as well as a physical one.

Simply looking into the idea of a Universal Power that is greater than yourselves, one that can be called upon and developed to help you through the rough times in your life, will foster a new idea of love within your heart. I certainly know there can be sex without love, but I'll tell you this: *Great* sex is born of love, and love for one another is partially born from the belief that a power greater than yourselves caused you to come together.

Putting an emphasis on some sort of spiritual renewal will in no way hamper or dampen the passion of your sexuality or your sensual longings, practices, and beliefs. It will enhance the meaning of human sexuality, what it's all about, and the treasure that has been given to you to use over and over again as often and as long as you desire.

Seeking New Places

One of the exciting things couples can do as they set this particular plank in place is seek a new place of worship together, maybe for the first time. I'm not suggesting that you abandon your own comfortable place of worship and particular faith, if you have one. But suppose you don't have those things? Wouldn't it be worthwhile, an adventure if you

will, to visit different churches or temples, to talk with min-
isters, priests, and rabbis who are not known to you?

It certainly would, and the emphasis on "adventure" cannot be too strong! You will enjoy looking at various services;
seeing other people and observing if they are experiencing
renewal of their own spiritual lives. That's what the two of
you are seeking. The place, the people, the practices, and
beliefs that help you break the molds of your past behavior
and enhance the quality of your life in sobriety.

When you are thinking about putting this plank in place
in your relationship bridge, please keep an open mind! Don't
automatically reject the idea out of hand. No one is going to
force you into doing something you don't want to do. However, risk-taking in this area, as well as in the areas that are
yet to come in this book, is vital if *things are going to be any
different*. I am only asking that you take the risk of investi-
gating this area of your life and consider the strength of this
plank in the bridge you are building.

If you are already established in a faith and in a place of
worship then you may be ahead of the game. What's ahead
for the two of you now is to take a long, hard look at what
you can do as a couple in the area of spiritual renewal. I have
seen couples who began teaching adult education or Sunday
school, or tried committee work together for a change, and
became really excited about seeing the way they worked
together.

"When I first asked Scott to help me teach the fourth-
grade Sunday school one Sunday," said Deb, "it was a real
turn-on for me. I never saw that side of him before. It was
like I had just discovered this hunk of a guy who could also
be caring, gentle, and so *good* with those kids! I had this
glimpse of being with an altogether different guy, and that's
what turned up my thermostat!"

Deb and Scott's experience is similar to that of many
couples. They had followed the plan of adding "spiritual
renewal" as an important blank in their relationship bridge.

It showed them that when they had taken the risk, they had discovered some new and different things about each other that were going to increase their sexual awareness of each other. Scott said, "Deb had always done this church bit on her own. I would rather play golf on Sundays. But she talked me into it because she got stood up by the teacher that was supposed to help her with this particular unit. I didn't really want to do it, but you know the more I worked in the same room with Deb, the more I became sort of aware of what a great woman she was . . . *is!*"

Scott continued, "She has a real knack with kids and I sort of got turned on to the idea that when we had a family, she was going to be a dynamite mother. That sort of made me take another look at Deb, instead of just taking her for granted like I did when I was drinking."

This young couple was willing to admit that they were seeing something in each other that they had not seen before. And what they were seeing, as plain and simple as it was, was beginning to enhance their relationship.

Seventh Plank: Sharing Chores

This may be one of the toughest planks to nail onto your bridge, but it's got to be done. For all of the work of the Women's Movement, the fact sadly remains that most men seem to be mired in stereotypical viewpoints that say, "Women deal with the house and kids, and men work!" The chauvinist has no place in building a new and productive relationship, and yet men are inclined to do just what they saw their fathers do.

Too many women, I fear, also put up with what their mothers did, and so we get into a real tug of war around the sharing of chores.

We all have to do certain chores to be able to co-exist, to live together. Even if we don't currently live together under one roof, we still have chores to do to make our dwellings habitable, comfortable, and inviting. But two sets of hands, legs, and backs working on these damn chores would leave a lot more time for the productive parts of our relationships. How much more time do you think the two of you could spend in making love and enjoying the new relationship of your sobriety if you weren't spending all your time on chores?

Housework and doing chores is a treadmill. Just after everything is cleaned you have to start doing it all over again. So why fight the system? Both of you pitching in to get the chores finished a little faster will certainly pay off later in the day when you want to spend the time or energy doing something else. So how do you divide up the stuff that has to be done?

Sit down together for breakfast in your favorite breakfast place. On a sheet of paper make two columns, headed "daily" and "weekly." Under "daily" would be things like make bed, load dishwasher, pick up after animals (if any), and so on. The so-called hard stuff, like laundry, vacuuming, bathrooms, kitchen floor, and windows, can be in the weekly column. Once you have listed all your chores, divide them between you. Both of you need to know what *has* to be done and then you start the "bidding" process. You decide who "doesn't mind" doing certain chores, and then put their name opposite that chore on your list.

Vary this assignment process on a weekly basis until you settle into something that is both fair, equitable, and, most of all, productive. The idea is to get this stuff done and get on to bigger and better things that advance the overall state of your relationship.

A good example revolves around laundry. Most men never seem to do laundry *exactly* the way their partner believes it should be done. That doesn't mean that men can't do laundry, it just means that they might beg off the chore and that their partner may let them beg off to avoid not "having it done right." Talk about it and devise a plan whereby you both understand how he or she wants their laundry handled and then do it that way.

If you do it the way your partner has requested then there is no potential argument. What you are always after in improving your relationship is to minimize the chances for argument. Laundry can also be done two or more times a week in little batches; that way it's not so overwhelming no matter who is assigned the chore.

You might even try using two separate laundry baskets. That way it's easy to keep whites and colored items separated during the week. Better yet, you can keep his and her laundry baskets. Makes doing laundry a snap and goes twice as fast.

You can divide up every chore in your house or houses this way, saving you both time, money, aggravation, and bickering. I have worked with couples who did not co-habitat who decided to clean each other's place on alternate weeks. They would both go to Sue's apartment and really get the place in A-one shape. Then they went to Dave's town house (where Sue really spent most of her time) and *both* worked on it.

This gave Sue the feeling that she was still caring for her things and made Dave seem more a part of her life. You can also "trade off" the chores that you really hate to do. Charles absolutely hated cleaning the kitchen, wouldn't even load the new dishwasher, preferring to leave the dirty dishes in the sink. On the other hand, Carol hated the weekly cleaning of the bathroom. Charles could do bathrooms "with one hand tied behind my back."

They switched these two jobs with each other and took them on as permanent assignments rather than changing weekly. It worked well for them, and they told me the chores were done a lot quicker because each knew how to do their task in an orderly and competent fashion. Instead of getting into bad moods, Charles and Carol started finding more time to spend on quality projects.

Housework is not a quality project; it is something that has to be done. Put aside your old prejudices and see how you can make this plank work in your new relationship bridge. I don't care if your dad never made the beds. What matters is what you want to do to share the chores that have to be done. Who cares whether your mother absolutely never did carpentry around the house? Does that mean you can't, even though you may be better at it than your male partner? Don't let ego get in the way—yours or his. If you can find more time to spend on other projects because you're perhaps better, faster, and more skilled than your male partner, then that is the criterion that should be used to get the chore done, not whether it fits a role model that doesn't work in your lives.

The sharing of chores does not just include housework, but obviously extends to the areas of child and animal care. Who says he always has to be the one to wash and clean out the cars? Who says she always has to change the diapers or make the formula?

If you find that a certain chore is being ignored, then head back to that breakfast table. Ask, "Is there some special reason why your chore(s) are not getting done?" And, "Do we need to look at the chore list again and make some changes? Seems like you're having a hard time around the [laundry] situation!" Or, "Do we need to do something different around the daily chore list? Looks like it's a problem for you to work on [loading the dishwasher] on a regular basis."

You might get into some territorial bickering when you first start dividing and doing chores, but it *will* smooth out if you keep in mind that the eventual payoffs are twofold: (1) Your place(s) will get and stay cleaned better and faster, and (2) With both of you handling the chores, there will be more time and energy to put into the relationship and into love-making!

MAKING SURE THE PLANKS FIT

It's very important that you and your partner examine the suggested planks again. Is there something you want to add or something you want to discard? You can do that as long as you keep in mind that these basic seven planks are common to all relationships, that I have found them to be tried and true in helping couples start a new bridge to a new relationship.

You can always modify, delete, or expand planks. Where you have special circumstances, where the plank doesn't quite seem to fit your bridge, change it. But keep the basic idea that it conveys. You have your own special old tapes, for example. How you begin to replace them will be uniquely yours; what's important is that you recognize the need to get rid of the old tapes and start playing new ones.

You may find it hard to deal with the plank "Forgetting as well as forgiving." But the work simply has to be done. Find the comfort level that the two of you can operate within and then do it. Verbalizing all the pitfalls in each plank will help both of you find the necessary extra elements that will keep your planks in place.

But whatever you do, don't discard the importance of nurturing your relationship to the overall goal of happier and more complete sex in sobriety. Your relationship is to be treated like a living and breathing entity all its own. If you do not water it and feed it and nurture it, it will perish. The things that you do for each other help to nurture the relationship.

When you were drinking, you were involved in a selfish mode of operating through life. It was a "Me, only" time. But now, in sobriety, you begin to think of the future. You begin to look not so much at how things are in your relationship but how things *can be*.

Looking at how things can be and examining the steps (planks) that you need to take to get there, automatically forces you to think of the other person in your life, and to be interested in building a new relationship with that person. It requires building a new relationship, for the old one was damaged or nearly destroyed by the use of alcohol and/or other drugs.

As your relationship grows and prospers, so, too, will the elements of your sexuality. For I firmly believe that you cannot separate one from the other. Ignore one, let it wither and die, and you starve and kill the other. Relationship-building and sexual promise are like Siamese twins, they cannot be separated.

Eight

Sexual Fantasy in Sobriety

Everyone retreats to a fantasy world at one time or another. Fantasy allows you to have the perfect job, to win the lottery, to find the perfect mate, the one who fulfills your dreams and whom you have sought in all the years of your most active sexuality.

THE CHILDHOOD FANTASIES

A great deal of our play as children is fantasy-oriented, and much of it fills the need to act out the sexually stereotypical roles to which we have been exposed. What little boy has not thrown an old piece of cloth around his shoulders, a mask over his eyes, and created a "superhero" of one kind or another? What little girl has not imagined herself the nurse who saves the stricken baby, or a princess who is rescued by a handsome prince? As you grow older your fantasies change, but fantasy remains a part of your life. When it comes to sexual experiences we first encounter the world of fantasy in self-exploration and masturbation. As children or even teens you may have occasional fantasies about your parents that are quickly condemned as "bad" or "unhealthy" by your conscience. If you have brothers or sisters, there is always the possibility that "exploring" has led to sexual exploration of each other's bodies—not necessarily anything more than "I'll show you mine if you show me yours."

This is in contrast to the many case of incest we hear about in the media. All too often, incest has been the product of alcohol and drug abuse by one or more members of the same family. Incest is a crime, not fantasy.

THE ROLE OF TRUE FANTASY

When you were drinking, many of the elements of your sex life were helped along, as it were, by the released inhibitions caused by alcohol. Fantasy was a much easier state for you to enter, either alone or with a partner.

You might even have played "sex games" where it was all right (while in a pretty well inebriated state) to pretend that you were other people. You might have been able to tell your sex partner that "it's okay to call me Bob" or whatever the name of an old boyfriend or ex-husband might have been. Your partner, equally befuddled by drink, participates in this sex fantasy, which might have given you an extra charge of sexual energy.

When it was over, however, when you both had sobered up, the remembrance of that episode could be a harmful weapon to be used against you.

USING FANTASY APPROPRIATELY

Fantasy is the opportunity, without alcohol, to explore the realms of each other's imaginations without the hurt so often attached to the fantasies used when you were drinking.

I recall treating a couple who had engaged in wild sexual fantasies of the "old girlfriend, old boyfriend" scenario that was a real turn-on for both of them. The problem arose when he stopped drinking for a period of time but she continued. During sex, she, without any urging this time from her partner, slipped into the same old fantasy roles they had played before. She called her partner by the name of her ex-husband and her current husband was suddenly unable to maintain his erection; he was angry, hurt, and jealous.

What had been okay when they were both drinking was now taboo, and boy, did she pay for it. He used that as a terrible weapon against her, accusing her of "not being through with her ex," and really still "wanting to be screwed by her ex," and so on and so forth—which is how they happened to end up in my office.

She felt she was being crucified for playing a game that had been such a turn-on when he was drinking along with her. They needed to find new uses for fantasy.

Fantasy can be a wonderful added value to your sex life in sobriety, and there are different ways that you can use it that won't be hurtful or harm the relationship, but rather can help nurture it and make it grow.

YOUR EROTIC LIFE

Fantasies feed the erotic part of your life.

Sex researcher Nancy Friday in her best-selling book *Men in Love,* says, "One of the great joys of the erotic experience should be the emotional freedom it confers for working toward separation, individuality, and independence."

In the past you used alcohol to gain emotional freedom, separation, individuality, and independence. And you may have liked it. Now the eroticism that grows from your fantasy can be used to rediscover the two of you, but in new and different, nonthreatening roles. The fantasies of the past won't work and must be abandoned for new ones.

Fits of all, let's look at selfish fantasies. Men who pored over *Playboy, Penthouse,* and the like might very well have gotten themselves excited by staring at naked women in various poses. Then what happened? They used their arousal state with the female they were with, imagining and fantasizing over the images they had been devouring.

They were, in effect, really just masturbating with a partner instead of sharing a wonderful emotional and physical experience. These men would think nothing of asking their partner to "pose like this girl," thrusting a huge color photo from a magazine at her. This is hardly the way to share sex; it is just a method of using a partner while fantasizing over the girl in the picture.

SEXUAL PUT-DOWNS

A kind of sexual put-down can happen when a man or woman makes comparisons between his or her fantasy and the person with whom they are sharing sex. A woman I was seeing in therapy a few years ago was a perfect example of this. Her lover was enamored of the singer Olivia Newton-John and obviously fantasized over her.

When in the throes of sexual excitement, while my patient was being undressed by her lover, he would shatter her entire sexual ego with a comment such as "Your legs aren't as good as Olivia Newton-John's, but they'll do." This woman was being used as no more than a symbol for his masturbation, which he was trying to pass off as "great sex."

Pornographic movies, so-called X-rated videos, are often used the same way. Usually the male partner wants to watch one of these extravaganzas and wants his companion to watch with him, thinking that this will be a great turn-on for them both. However, it has the opposite effect on most women, who begin to feel that "I'm not good enough for him; he needs to be stimulated by watching other women."

Interestingly enough, national statistics released in the spring of 1990 showed that more women were renting these kinds of videotapes than before—that is, the percentage of rentals to women as reported by video-rental stores was on the increase.

Does this mean that women's ideas around fantasy and

sex are changing? I doubt it. I rather believe that more women are simply including a stop at the video store to pick up these tapes at the request of their male partner and feel less shy about doing so.

There is nothing in my experience to suggest that the basic idea of a woman watching men make love to other women is much of a turn-on. Mostly, it is a simple case of voyeurism, a method to get sensual satisfaction from just looking. The trouble begins when, somewhere in the middle of the video, the man starts grabbing for his partner and wants to "get it on."

Is this man turned on and peaking to a high degree of sexual desire because of the woman he is with? More likely he is turned on by the images he is seeing on the screen and then using his companion to act out the fantasy. Thus it just becomes another sexual put-down that neither of you need.

It's the same thing with the reading of "sexy" books. This has most often been a singular activity that either you or your partner have practiced, and therefore the fantasies that may have been born from these books were not really shared with your love partner but probably acted out by you and urged on by the alcohol or drugs you were consuming.

Take away the alcohol and the drugs and you have possibly become downright embarrassed to act out the fantasies that you have read.

NEW TECHNIQUES ARE NEEDED

What's called for now are new techniques—not new in that I created them but new in your thinking and *definitely* new in your sexual practices without alcohol.

There certainly needs to be joy in sober sex, and so the things that I am going to describe for you are based on what I know has been successful in the past with hundreds of couples who have tried them. Don't automatically reject them. Don't say to yourself or to your partner, "I've/we've tried that!" I don't care if you tried it before; remember that *before* also included drinking or drugging.

YOUR SEXUAL RESPONSIBILITY

You have a responsibility for your own sexual satisfaction and pleasure. It is not something that you can lay off on your partner and therefore accuse him or her of not "doing the right things" to you or with you when you are having sexual experiences. The six specific "game plans" or "projects" that you are going to learn can bring sober joy into your sex lives. They are projects that will also help you take responsibility for your own sexuality.

The business of being responsible for your own pleasure was dynamically presented several years ago in a workshop given by a husband and wife psychologist team, Marilyn and Bill Simon, who live and practice in New York. I was one of perhaps fifty therapists attending this particular workshop on sexuality. Marilyn divided the therapists into two long lines of twenty-five each, which she designated Line A and Line B.

Since this was the first session of the day, not too many people knew each other, but everyone was wearing a tradi-tional "Hello" name tag.

Marilyn had Line A facing the members of Line B in no particular order. You just stood opposite whoever was there. Line A was given a sentence on a piece of paper. Then Bill Simon announced over the microphone that he wanted Line A to say the sentence that had been given to them. Here was the sentence.

"Hello. My name is _____ , and I'm totally responsible for my own orgasm!"

After the laughter settled down from *both* lines, Bill had Line A repeat the phrase, over and over, using whatever different inflections a person cared to use. When it seemed that this phrase had been indelibly drummed into the person opposite, the Simons ordered Line A to shift one person over to the right.

Now, you were facing another total stranger who was either male or female. The same phrase was spoken again and again to this new person! The exercise continued until all of the therapists in that room had clearly gotten the message: *"You* are totally responsible for your *own* orgasm!"

It was a good lesson and one I've passed along many times to my own patients. There is little ground for blaming your partner for your sexual dysfunction. Those were behaviors that you used to either drink more or as reasons to drink in the first place. How often has the phrase been used, and sometimes viciously, "I wouldn't have to drink if she/he were better in bed."

If each person is completely responsible for his or her own sexual satisfaction (orgasm as an all-encompassing description), then it stands to reason that blaming the partner is definitely out, particularly in sobriety and in being clean from drugs.

THE SIX PROJECTS

Here, then, are the six projects that you and your partner are going to practice as a means of improving and changing the ways in which you have been sexually involved. These are *sober* sexual techniques, and if used and practiced over and over will far surpass anything that alcohol or drugs ever created in the way of sexual highs.

1. The shared bath
2. The shared massage
3. Creative photography
4. Shared books and pictures
5. Home video production
6. Character roles

When you have gone through these and practiced and used the techniques I have given you, then by all means, expand the list. That's where fantasy really begins to work and where you can use your imaginations to plan strategy and move the pieces of your sexuality around the board of your relationship. Above all, enjoy these things! A word of caution, however: It is important that both of you be comfortable in doing the projects. If one is uncomfortable, stop and go on to something else.

You may have some failures; some of the exercises just won't feel right for you, but variations on them all work. So take the basics that I give you and expand, ad-lib, improvise, and build, keeping the basic framework that I have outlined. The books that I will be referring to are listed in the bibliography at the end of this book.

The books listed have been chosen for several reasons but mostly because they are readily available (most are in paperback), and can be added to your permanent collections to be used over and over again. Others are available as reference works from your library and can be used by the more serious student or person interested in the clinical data that surrounds sexuality and alcohol and drug abuse.

Above all, please keep an open mind! If you begin to read just a little and then discard either what I'm saying or what someone else is writing, then you are owning defeat, believing that your sexual life will not change now that you are in sobriety. If that happens to you, then only you and your partner are the losers.

Many of the things I will be suggesting might, at first glance, appear to be expensive projects; they are not. In fact, everything that I will be suggesting will be available to you for considerably less than you ever spent in pursuing your drinking or drugging. If a necessary item is *absolutely* not available to you, then put your imagination to work and substitute something that will give the same effect.

The only boundaries here are the ones you set. Don't rush any of these creative projects. Set aside the time and the energy they require. The art of making sober love requires the nurturing element in a relationship that can't be hurried.

They key to all of this is to share and not to be involved in only selfish pursuits—that just won't work.

If you can't plan the several hours that are necessary for some of these "projects" then don't even start them; wait until you can take the time, free from other pressures, to practice and enjoy them. It sounds ridiculous that you may have to practice having wonderful sexual experiences, but that's exactly what you have to do. You have little or no experience in having rewarding sex without the use of an alcoholic or drug crutch.

Finally, keep in mind that there is really little or nothing new in the field of sex education, so don't be expecting that you are going to be on the ground floor of startling revelations. What I will be giving you are techniques and variations of sexual approaches that loving couples can share, unafraid that they will fail because they have no alcohol or drug to keep them stimulated, interested, and capable of being the lover they have fantasized being.

FANTASY FOR SINGLES

The six projects that I am going to detail were, admittedly, designed for couples, whether heterosexual or gay/lesbian. If you are single you may feel left out. Please don't. Your fantasies are no different since you use them to reach orgasm, the same reason couples use fantasy.

You can still perform many of the fantasy projects yourself, using your own props and settings to help you be autoerotic, to achieve in masturbation a finer and more complete sense of self, one that is no longer numbed by alcohol or strung out on drugs to the point that little sexual stimulation worked or was even desired when compared to the need and desire for more booze or drugs, despite the strength of your fantasies. Those days and nights are now passed.

Experiment with yourself. Learn to be comfortable with your own body in a sober state and notice how much more pleasure you feel, and how sensitive to your own touch you have become. You need to take the time and make the effort to achieve climax, yes, but also to experience that tranquillity and real sense of the sensual person you are, and *always have been*, before alcohol or other drugs took away your senses and numbed your feelings.

BEFORE YOU START THE PROJECTS

There are some ground rules about doing these projects. They must be satisfactory to *both* of you or they should not be used. You will, however, not be able to determine if they are useful unless you try them, so you are not allowed (by the rules) to give up any of these projects until you have tried them. If one of you becomes uncomfortable, stop and talk about why that particular project is not working. When you find projects that work for you, I want to hear about it, anonymously if you like. What I want to know is:

What "projects" worked best?
Did you feel your fantasies could be realized?
What variations did you try?
What new projects did you and your partner create?
Did using the projects help you overcome sexual hang-
    ups that you had overcome before with alcohol or
    drugs?

Write to me:

Jack Mumey
Gateway Treatment Center
1191 South Parker Road, Suite 100
Denver, CO 80231

If you do sign your name, I assure you that your reply will be held strictly confidential, though your ideas might find themselves in a future book!

I'll let Dr. Alex Comfort, general editor of the very popular *The Joy of Sex*, set the tone for following the projects: "There are only two guidelines in good sex, 'Don't do anything you don't really enjoy,' and 'Find out your partner's needs and don't balk at them if you can help it.' "

Nine

A New Road to
Intimacy

Fantasy is important in sexual behavior because it helps
transport a person, and possibly a partner, into realms where
their imagination sets the guidelines for behavior, the boundaries that will mark their sexual behavior.

To further enhance the idea of fantasy and help you
explore your own sexuality without the use of alcohol or
drugs, we are going to take a new road to intimacy by in-
troducing "projects" that you can do, alone and together, for
the further enhancement of a sober sex life.

These are projects with equal payoffs as the goal for both
partners. This isn't something that you are going to enjoy
alone, forgetting about the pleasure of your partner. This is
something that you are going to do *together*, because that's
what makes the project work, in addition to what makes it
fun.

In each of the projects, you will have a list of the basic
materials needed; substitute as closely as you can if you find
that you don't have exactly what is called for in the list.

COMFORT LEVELS

None of these projects will work if you are feeling uncomfortable about them. They have been designed to help you gain more intimacy, but if you are fighting the basic structure of the project in the first place, then you will never reap the benefit of the project's payoffs.

Look at them carefully, and then decide if it's something you want to try. You don't have to worry about rejecting anything, but it would be best if you studied the possibilities thoroughly before rejecting the project out of hand.

Talk the project over with your partner, see what his/her comfort level seems to be, and talk openly about the possibilities of doing the project; listen carefully to objections, if any, and then see if you need to modify some part of the project in order to make it more acceptable.

You are being asked to take some risks with your sexuality, but they are risks that have been taken by many of my patients and have provided excellent results from the feedback that has been given me.

THE SHARED BATH

The purpose of this project is to help you improve communications with your partner on a level that may not have occurred before. Specifically, using this project as a part of the foreplay to sexual intercourse, a project that requires your spending some quality time together in a soothing, relaxing atmosphere. The items needed are:

Bathtub (not hot tub; *not* shower)
Lots of candles
Bubble bath, baby oil, body lotion
Music source
Iced fruit juices (sparkling apple juice)
Small platter of cheeses, sausage, apple, pear slices, crackers

You may already be setting up a howl of protest that I am eliminating the shower for this project, but that's the way it's going to be. There is very little that is soothing about taking a shower together; stimulating, yes, soothing, no. Also, the shower tends to focus on the grabbing of breasts and genitals, whereas the tub project is designed for sharing a relatively small space together, forcing you to concentrate more on the closeness of one another rather than on individual body parts.

How big a tub? If two of you can manage to get into it, then it's big enough, but if yours really won't work, you need to consider going to a motel or hotel that has one. When you were drinking you would have gone anywhere to do what you wanted, so there should be nothing stopping you from giving the same priority to *sober* sex games.

I'm not suggesting that you spend a lot of money. If you are a couple that can't fit into your own tub, then going to a motel or hotel might only be a periodic project. Either way, let's assume that you have found a tub that works. The next step is to make sure all the equipment needed is in place; don't keep getting in and out of the tub because you "forgot something."

If you want to add to the equipment list things like headrest pillows, feel free to do so. Sometimes a little bamboo fan to keep yourselves from sweating is nice. With two of you in a tub warm enough to make the bubble bath work, the temperature in the bathroom will increase considerably.

Obviously, no kids or pets are allowed in with you. This is for you two alone. If a radio is your music source, make sure it is far away from the tub itself to avoid the possibility of electrocution. Inexpensive, battery-powered "shower radios" work really well, as does music from another room that is loud enough to be heard in the bathroom. Make sure the music is truly *background*, and not something you need to shout over.

Face each other in the tub. Experiment with whose legs

need to rest on whose, and get as comfortable as possible, just as long as you are facing each other. Only candles should light the room, no other illumination. So-called novena candles that come in boxes of a dozen and are available at most craft stores are great for this. They are cheap and you can use bunches of them around the tub, on nearby shelves, counters, or on the tub edges themselves.

In the tub, with the music softly playing in the background and the candles providing soft light, begin to get comfortable just being together—without grabbing for each other. Nice, gentle soaping of your partner is suggested, letting the bubble bath soap cling as you dab at your partner with a washcloth, sponge, or even just cover them with the bubbles from the bath.

No touching of genitals at this point, please. Pour each other a glass of fruit juice. I recommend the sparkling apple juice for a tangy, refreshing drink. Feed each other some of the cheese, apple slices, and crackers and sausage.

Now comes the hard part. As you begin to let the soothing bath water relax you, start to talk. Ask your partner how his day was and *listen* to his answer. You can also talk about other people, places, things. You can discuss anything *except* hard problem areas: finances, in-laws or other disagreeable relatives, discipline problems, major argument starters. None of those have a place in your romantic bath interlude.

What I would like you to concentrate on is noticing one another: how nice it is to be sober, to be this close; how nice her skin feels; how nice he looks to you; how you had forgotten that it was good to be *this close*. This project is simply an exercise in closeness, nothing more or less. When you are comfortable with this closeness then you can begin a sober foreplay to what may come later.

When one of you was drinking there wasn't really much time spent in lovemaking; either you wanted to drink more than you wanted to make love, or you were unable to be on the giving end of the relationship. I know I'm making some generalizations about the state of the drinking relationship, but I have seen enough couples in therapy to know that those relationships were of a selfish nature and not of the sharing kind that I'm getting you to try.

Letting Troubles Dissolve

The idea of the shared bath is to let the troubles of the day/week dissolve away as your comfort each other, to let the warm and soothing water melt away the aches, pains, and cares of the workaday world. At the same time, the shared bath serves as a prelude to the lovemaking that may come later, either immediately following the bath or later that evening.

Either way, the emphasis is on *sharing, soothing, sensual* soaking. Get out when you're ready and gently towel each other dry, with the emphasis on *gently*. Take your time and feel how relaxed your partner's body is and how it responds to your touch. Use the baby oil or lotion on each other, smoothing the skin and feeling with the touch and scent of the lotion or oil.

After applying the oil, and if you are going to dress for the moment, towel the excess off your partner's body. Dress in loose robes or kimonos, even just two men's shirts with underwear will do; anything to protect the feelings of the bath you have just finished.

As we leave the Shared Bath, keep in mind that improvisation is your best tool. Make do with what you have; let your fantasy abound and make your imagination loose. Doing the Shared Bath takes preparation and some planning to make the most of it, but the payoffs are tremendous. As you go along, you'll find yourself looking forward to your bath whether it's weekly, bimonthly, or monthly.

Even when you travel together, you can find the time and the ingenuity to make this project work. The important thing is to make it a solid part of your sober relationship, something that becomes a bridge to a better relationship all by itself because it promotes togetherness and the sensuality of touching.

Don't reject this project out of hand. All of these activities may seem a little strange to you; after all, your fantasies were all wrapped up with alcohol, so working on sober fantasies will be just that, work, until you begin to see the payoffs.

In one of our couples group therapies, I had each of the four couples in the group work on the Shared Bath. The couple who had been the first to "take the plunge," so to speak, reported back to the group on how wonderful the experiment had been. The man in particular said that he was "completely amazed" at how wonderful the communications had been between him and his partner as they shared a tub.

Everyone in the group gave the couple a great deal of warm feedback for their bravery and their openness in sharing the experience. It was only later that I learned we were not getting the whole story. In spite of my detailed instructions (the same as I have given here), the man in question had made one small change.

"Yeah, it was wonderful being alone," his wife confided, "if you consider there was just the two of us, the candles, and the whole damn Boston Celtic basketball team!"

Our friend, not finding a portable radio, brought in a portable TV and had a Celtic game on during their "romantic bath." It all turned out okay because I urged the lady to share this important news with the rest of the group, which she did the following week. Her partner was duly chastised by his peers and said he certainly realized that he had made a mistake.

He insisted, however, that the "communications and the romance" had really started to be better. They continued their weekly baths, minus the Celtics, and sure enough, things got a whole lot better, so much so that when they missed the Shared Bath for a couple of weeks because of work schedule changes, they noticed the difference in their attitudes toward each other, and in the tempo of their sexual activity. When the baths resumed, the sexual activity increased and became more satisfactory for both.

"Funny," they both said, "taking a bath together was something we were more likely to do when George was drinking, but it was horrible the one or two times we tried it. Now, it's *beautiful*."

The Bath for Singles

Everything that I have outlined for couples will work for singles. The purpose is to give you a sense of your own body, to allow you to relax in a warm tub with the bubbles all around you.

Use your imagination and sexual fantasies in self-stimulation. Let the cares of the day float away and substitute the warm, scented oil of the bath for the wine or beer or shot of vodka you may have used in the past.

Autoeroticism or masturbation is a healthy and perfectly normal activity. The luxurious bath will help transport you in your flights of fancy, will help make you feel good about yourself and about your body, no matter what shape you may be in at the moment.

THE SHARED MASSAGE

This may or may not be a continuation of the above exercise. It really needs to stand alone as a project because it can be done quite independent of anything else. You will need:

Large towels or covers to protect the bed (If you have a futon, you can use that instead of the bed.)
Body lotion, baby oil, scented oil but no rubbing alcohol
Music source
Candles

You will begin to notice that candles play a large role in all of these projects. They add to the sensuality of the scene, and they soften the hardest of lines, helping to set the mood for softness and luxury even when the actual surroundings aren't.

You may choose to use both a scented oil and a body lotion, or give your partner some options as to which he or she would prefer. If you can heat the oil and bring it to the massage location safely and easily then do so. Don't do any more than make it slightly over tepid, otherwise it will burn you both. The towels or covers are to protect the bed, or wherever you are giving the massage, from the oil or lotions.

The location doesn't have to be the bedroom. In fact, one of the great things about fantasy is that the setting can be anywhere you want; try spreading sleeping bags (well covered to protect them) on the floor in front of the fireplace in the living room or the den.

Use your imagination. How about the couch or sofa? Even a big chair or lounger; a chaise lounge, bench, or pool table; or what about the kitchen or dining room table, where the surface can be made comfortable and protected.

In other words, let your fantasies run the gamut, share ideas for locations with your partner and agree to "give it a try" with the understanding that you may not wish to repeat that particular location again. The willingness to communicate your fantasies with each other adds to the charm of each of these projects and must not be laughed at or scorned but entered into in the spirit with which they are designed.

Even though I have not included particular books in the "needed" list, I am assuming that you will read them together as part of the Shared Books and Pictures project. The more familiar you become with Dr. Kassorla's *Nice Girls Do* and the popular *The Art of Sensual Massage* by Gordon Inkeles and Murray Todris, the more you will want to include their suggestions as you give your own sensual massages.

As Inkeles and Todris write, "Touch is the oldest and truest form of communion. Work through this book with a lover or friend. It's going to teach you a new way of touching and being touched."

A British work, Dr. Andrew Yorke's *The Art of Erotic Massage*, is extremely well photographed and is helpful for technique-learning skills.

A Prelude to Lovemaking

The Shared Massage is designed for both of you to begin to feel each other again, unhampered by the constrictions of either alcohol or some other drug.

You are going to begin gently massaging first one and then the other, having in mind only to give comfort, pleasure, rest, relaxation, and a sense of security and safety to your partner. Those last two items are really important. In all of your sexual activity in sobriety, the idea of always being in a safe and secure place with your partner is primary.

This means *no laughing* at attempts, bungled or successful; it means that you are willing to engage in these activities with an open mind and a willingness to share the experiences so as to build a new, strong, vibrant, *sober* relationship. If either of you feels unsafe and insecure, then the project will fail.

Once again, consider the Shared Message as a prelude to your lovemaking but not necessarily a requirement for it. I believe that you should learn to use the massage as a means of general improvement in your relationship as well as the endless possibilities it holds for the sexual and sensual part of your lives.

Treat the massage primarily as *sensual* even though you may be trying "erotic massage." The purpose of these shared massages is to teach you the joy of giving comfort, of "healing" by the "laying on of hands" with love and compassion for your partner.

As the muscles begin to relax under your gently kneading fingers, your partner begins to develop a sense of well-being. The sensuality of warm oil flowing over the skin, directed by you, is most conducive to arousal, but don't make that the end-all of the massage.

Like the Shared Bath, the Shared Massage project is designed for you to be willing to give something of yourself without expecting something in return. You each benefit by being both the *giver* of the massage as well as the *receiver*. Neither of you will receive a bigger payoff than the other.

Taking Proper Time

Both of you must be willing to take the time necessary to truly relax the other person, even though your very touching of him or her might be leading to strong, erotic arousal.

The trick is for you to keep those feelings in check for the moment and simply learn to feel the beauty of your partner's body. How marvelous it will be for you to really sense his or her skin with your fingertips; fingertips that had probably lost their sense of finite touch through alcohol abuse.

You see, the more you used alcohol the more you became anesthetized, losing your senses of touch and smell. To be successful in this project you must be willing to give at least thirty minutes to it. About fifteen minutes of massage for each partner will relax you and allow you to shake off the cares of the workday, to help you "shift gears" into the romance of the evening.

Don't try to engage in conversation; it isn't necessary. Just let the music and the candlelight carry the moment, supplemented with the caress of your hands on your partner's body. As in the Shared Bath, no probing, fondling, or anything except genuine massage of the body is allowed! No playing with genitals, no deliberate arousal of nipples even though this will naturally occur as part of the massage with oil or lotion.

Your purpose here is not to stimulate your partner but to relax him or her and to share the joy of gentle caress as a token of love and care of his or her well-being. It will be hard for you to leave your partner alone sexually, but *do* it, until you are able to give and take the Shared Massage as a gift.

Continuing Down the Path of Intimacy

In her book *Forbidden Flowers,* Nancy Friday says, "Summoning up an erotic image in the imagination does not necessarily mean we want to bring it into reality. In fact, very often the fantasy itself discharges the forbidden energy and entirely eschews the need for acting it out."

Dr. Joe LoPiccolo has a message that applies to those heading down this new road to intimacy regardless of whether you are walking it as a couple or as a single person: "Fantasizing about something does not mean that you will actually do it. In fact, the beauty of fantasy is that it allows you the freedom to experiment with sexual variety beyond the limits of reality."

We cannot repeat too often, remind ourselves too frequently, that sex in a state of sobriety is entirely different, new, and many times more frightening because all the inhibitions that may have been temporarily blocked by alcohol have probably come back to haunt you.

The use of fantasy and these projects will help you on the road to establishing new ways, new ideas, new techniques to a satisfying and exciting sexual relationship with that special partner in your life; all without drinking or taking some other kind of drug. As a single, the exploration of your own body, the comfort level of touching and massaging yourself, is greatly enhanced without the alcohol or the drug to numb the delicious feel of your own hands upon the largest organ of the human body, the skin.

CREATIVE PHOTOGRAPHY

You will need:

A Polaroid or 35mm camera
Candles (the more the merrier!)
Outdoor settings
Large door mirror
Music

Let me stress emphatically that *none* of these projects is designed to get you into anything kinky or necessarily even offend your dignity. However, they *are* designed to test your imagination, to stretch your fantasies and to realize that your own sexuality *and* sensuality has for the most part been untapped. You haven't really been allowed to escape the hold the old relationship with alcohol had on you and your partner. These projects are a means of breaking those holds.

Photography as a Stimulant

The use of photography to excite and stimulate you and to increase the ability of your relationship to grow is unparalleled, not to mention the ease and general low cost involved. The problem has been that most of the photography that you probably have come in contact with has been of some other man or woman, and not of the endless fantasies possible with your own partner.

If you are female, you have had the debilitating experience, I am sure, of seeing copies of "girlie" magazines around your partner's place. Kind of made you decide that you couldn't or wouldn't try to compete, right? Or, it made you so damned angry that any thought of a great sexual encounter went out the window.

If you are male, you might have seen photo layouts of "hunks" in the tabloids or sensational magazines; even popular women's magazines that might have some pretty explicit photos of male stars. Tell me, how did you feel about *those?*

Society has maintained extreme double standards in the past. Today, however, women emphatically tell the male world that there is a sexual quid pro quo. If men are going to continue to gape at women's bodies, then women are going to have magazines and books of their own to look at, with naked and seductively posed men to fan women's fantasies.

It is very damaging to a relationship for one partner or

the other to hold up comparisons, something that's "better" about someone else in the hopes that your partner will make the changes necessary to match your ideal.

Looking at Your Partner

In Creative Photography, we are going to forget what other people look like and capture on film what you and your partner look like. The collection of photographs that the two of you take can be part of the Shared Books and Pictures project that follows this one. But more than that, they can become an ever-growing source of experimentation and free-wheeling imagination, all born from the shared fantasies of both of you.

To make it work, both of you have to *trust* your partner's fantasies. Fantasies are safe encounters that are perfectly normal. If a female fantasizes about group sex, it certainly does not mean she wants to take part in an orgy; it simply means she is using such a fantasy as a means of gaining a variety of sexual partners in her imagination, partners that may cause more creative energy to flow into the sexual relationship she is enjoying in the real world, with a real lover.

Certainly a man fantasizing about watching his partner being ravished by another man does *not* mean he wants this to happen in real life. He is merely exercising the voyeuristic nature of his sexuality.

When you use photography, you are again participating in a form of foreplay to whatever sexual experiences may follow. Before you start, you must both agree that it will be "fun" to take pictures of each other. If it isn't fun for both of you, then don't do it.

When you were drinking, or when your partner was drinking, you may have taken photos together. However, if you saved them and look at them now, you will see people who were not real, not clear-eyed or alert. In fact, you may actually be disgusted by such photos because they are more a reminder of the slavery of alcohol than of the sensuality they were supposed to portray.

Starting Fresh

You should start fresh—and *easy*. Perhaps you can find a spot in the mountains, at a park, or at the beach in an area secluded enough so you don't have to worry about someone invading your privacy. Or you can do this project in the privacy of your home. Just be sure you won't be interrupted by kids or neighbors. Select your spot, then begin by *photographing each other* in the same stage of undress. If you want a picture of your female companion with her shirt or blouse unbuttoned, then you give her the same opportunity.

In this manner you proceed to take a series of semi-nude photographs, always ready to quit if either party begins to feel uncomfortable. Remember, if you did this before it was probably when you were drinking or drugging, so you had a built-in buffer to the experience.

The use of a Polaroid allows you to do other creative and fairly exotic picture-taking. A simple sequence of one of you undressing and stepping into a tub of bubbles can produce an entire fantasy sequence as you "direct" the action for your partner to follow. This may be acting out a fantasy of yours to "surprise" someone in their bath preparations. It'll work for the female if she just changes the setting slightly, perhaps like this:

You are a woman, and your fantasy has been that your partner is in the garage finishing work on the car. (Click!) He becomes hot and begins to remove his shirt (click!), then he sits on the edge of the workbench and takes off his boots (click!) and pants (click!), and, finally, is found going into the shower (click!) where you are free to (click! click!) to your heart's content as he showers.

Using Life Situations

A simple life situation is always the best to make a sequence like this, and anyone can do it. You have endless possibilities of creating a little "mini-series," and you'll find it stimulating and fun to try.

Bedroom photography, utilizing mirrors, candles, and music will indeed "put you in the mood," but be careful not to rush these photo sessions. Take your time, as in all the things in your relationship rebuilding. It will pay off in the long run. Again, make sure each partner gets *equal* time with the camera.

If you use a 35mm camera where the film is generally developed by a lab, make certain that you are okay with having you privacy invaded by strangers. The Polaroids are so inexpensive, they make an ideal camera for you to have and use, and you keep the whole scene to yourselves; however, I included both sources because you have much more photographic abilities and latitudes with a 35mm than with the less expensive, fixed focus Polaroid.

Singles Using Pictures

There is a sense of wonderment and awe to a person who sees themselves in a photograph naked or in some stage of undress. And you can enjoy this even if you're single. The trick is to use your camera on yourself by standing in front of a full-length mirror. If you are using a Polaroid, you can photograph a provocative breast; a curved, stockinged leg; or a navel with a belt that has been loosened and pants partially lowered.

Self-timing devices on more expensive cameras will allow you to put your camera on a tripod, set the timer, and then stand or lie in the position that you have chosen. Have mood-setting music playing, candles in position, and the fastest speed film you can get for your camera.

In the Polaroid, the 600-type film works very well. Just

be careful not to let the built-in flash be seen in the mirror. Hold the camera so you can't see it in the mirror, then the mirror obviously won't reflect it.

SHARED BOOKS AND PICTURES
Select at least some of these:

> *The Joy of Sex* by Alex Comfort
> *More Joy* by Alex Comfort
> *Delta Venus* by Anais Nin
> *The Photographic Guide to Sexual Secrets* by Sean O'Connor
> *Intercourse Illustrated* by Walter Braun, M.D.
> *Nice Girls Do* by Irene Kassorla, Ph.D.
> *How to Make Love All the Time* by Barbara DeAngelis, Ph.D.
> *Love Skills, a Guide to the Pleasures of Sex*, video
> Your own photos
> *Playboy's Secrets of Euromassage,* video
> *Pretty Woman*, video movie

Sharing these things is definitely an important "must" in your new thinking and acting about your sexual revolution — sex without alcohol, that is. Too much of your past sexual experiences were really not shared. He did what he wanted; you did what you wanted — and probably neither of you shared either fantasies or expectations about what you wanted from the other.

In Shared Books and Pictures, not only are you going to look at and read things together, but you are gong to *discuss* them as well. It isn't boring, so trust the process, please. Most of the books on the list can be purchased at reasonable cost either in local bookstores or through mail-order houses such as Publishers Central Bureau (see complete list at end of book). The movies can be rented, of course, or purchased if you prefer.

Reading Together

Your own pictures taken over several weeks are also included in the list. Going over them together can be very stimulating and enlightening. Read the Alex Comfort books in bed perhaps, discussing the text and the pictures. With *Delta Venus*, *Nice Girls Do*, and *How to Make Love All the Time*, you can take turns reading a chapter aloud once a week or more often if you both desire to do so. Don't force any of this; take it all in stride as part of the natural rebirth of your sexual life together.

Be willing to talk about things you see in the pictures or read in the text that you don't understand. You should not be threatened by your lack of knowledge about something sexual; as humans we are woefully ignorant of many things relating to our own sexuality.

Asking Questions

When you are looking at the pictures, ask questions of one another. "Do we want to try this?" or "How would you feel doing this?" will come up a lot between the two of you. Be honest in your answers. If you see or read about something that makes you very uncomfortable, or if you detect a sense of not liking what is being said or described, then say so.

You might reject something at first, but in discussing it with your partner you might decide to give it at try. Look at the pictures that the two of you have made and use them to build new fantasy stories for you to share. For example, you might ask her what she was *really* thinking when you were photographing and "directing" her bath sequence.

Maybe she will let you in on a new fantasy that little sequence triggered in her, an episode you might want to act out in photographs again. As you review together the pictures that you have taken, new sequences can be talked about.

In looking at the materials in the books, experiment with

some of the positions they illustrate even if you are not going to have sex! Once again, learning to control impulse is going to be new for you, and I am not saying that you will always be successful in control. If you are not, then so much the better, for you will then be involved in a new and hopefully rewarding act of making love together, without the stimulation of alcohol.

Mutually Sharing

The question now obviously arises, "Is there any difference between getting 'turned on' by looking at pictures and reading books than by drinking?" Well, sure there is. The biggest is that you remain in control before, during, and after sex, even though you may experience marvelous abandonment during sex. When the alcohol was a factor, too often you neither remembered nor wanted to remember what had happened.

The second and biggest point is that when you are reading books together, when you are looking at your pictures together, and when you are trying to experiment together, you are then *sharing* the sexual experience as opposed to just one of you taking and the other one giving. Like it or not, there is an underlying selfish motif that is present in alcohol-induced lovemaking sessions.

In selecting the videos for you to watch, I had a definite criteria that had to be met before I could recommend them to you. I have also "tested" these films (and others) on other couples and feel that they most clearly meet the objectives of relationship rebuilding that I am always stressing—not just sex, *relationships*.

What are the criteria? Well, probably the best thing about all of these videos is that they all "turn out good," as a friend of mine says. There are good feelings that you get when you watch them; even *Love Skills* is upbeat and tasteful, although very explicit in showing sexual positions and the acting out of several fantasies for both men and women.

Another point for recommendation is that they are instructive, even if they are entertainment.

Pretty Woman is a wonderful example of how change can benefit a relationship, how a relationship that has absolutely nothing going for it except "buy and sell" can be built from the stereotypical into the unexpected. So the third point in my criteria is "taking risks/making changes."

Not only are these films great entertainment, but they are erotic in their own way; some of it being quite subtle, some of it hitting you over the head with a sledgehammer, but at least portrayed in a definite "see this with someone you love" manner.

If you have other films that you think capture the spirit of what we are doing in these projects, then use them; let me know the titles and what made you choose them. My list is only a starter, but be sure that you keep focused on the idea that these are books, pictures, and films that you use together, and if any of these materials don't work that way, then they are out.

Expressing Doubts and Fears

I realize that many of you are very sophisticated about sex; maybe you have used the techniques I'm giving you and feel that there is nothing more for you to learn. But think of this: For many of you, just talking about having sex in sobriety is one of the most feared topics. And, of course, *doing* it is even scarier.

I have had people confess that they have relapsed because of their fears about having sex or about being rejected by the opposite sex, and by feeling that they could not live up to the expectations of their partners in a state of sobriety. It is certainly one of the biggest factors in relapse that gets cited by patients who must now begin the road to recovery from square one because they returned to drinking, fearing their sexuality.

That's why this idea of Shared Books and Pictures is so

important in our project plan. It is a concrete way to have several vehicles, including the photographs you took of each other, to expressing even some of the doubts and fears that have probably crept into the dark recesses of your mind about sex in sobriety.

Asking Questions of Each Other

Sharing books and pictures and watching videos together opens the way for conversation about the topic itself. Be okay with finally asking these questions of each other:

How is sex with me sober?
Do you feel different about me sexually now?
What seems harder to do now?
What seems easier to do now?
Has your sexual desire slipped or increased? (Ask this even if you know the answer!)
Can you tell me what you like? Dislike?
Are you afraid of sex with me now? Why?
What can we do to make it better?
Do you want to drink (use drugs) again?
How can I specifically help the way you feel?

The last question is particularly tough because every person has a right to feelings and you can't or shouldn't accept responsibility for how they feel. If your partner is feeling as if he or she can't live up to your expectations about sex, he or she is entitled to feel that way but not entitled to keep you from trying to make changes in yourself that would help.

In other words, you are not trying to deny your partner's feelings, but you will do everything possible to prevent your partner from keeping the luxury of just drowning in those feelings and not letting you throw out a lifeline. Try talking over these questions and being honest in the answers. Again, do them together as part of this exercise in the project of Shared Books and Pictures.

The more you sit or lie together in bed and share the books, the pictures, the films, and the photos, the more you will enrich the entire sexual process of being in sobriety. It's worth the risks of "exposure."

MORE DIFFICULT PROJECTS

These last projects may seem a little difficult at first. Remember that you are in a learning mode. You are going to try these things *without* drinking or drugging. Once again, keep in mind these "projects" are all relationship-building devices, designed to help share your fantasies and to rebuild a relationship.

HOME VIDEO PRODUCTION

You will need:

Any video camcorder of any format or make
A standard camera tripod
Music from any source *except* television
Candles (plenty of them)

This project involves producing your own videos of the two of you doing all sorts of wonderful things with each other. The key ingredient here is that you will not be watching some professional porno "stars," but you will be watching you and your partner in the act of making love.

When I have couples try this at home they are very reluctant at first, fearing that they will suddenly be "embarrassed" by seeing themselves, or that someone else will accidentally get hold of the tape. Put all that out of your mind.

First, you should be no more embarrassed than seeing yourselves in the mirror when you might have been doing your still photography sessions. Second, if you and your partner don't have a secure place for your private, intimate things, then *anything* you might do or have is subject to invasion. Get a safe place—a locked drawer, a closet, a desk—where you can keep your pictures, tapes, books, or whatever you may collect in these projects.

Making Your First Tape

As you gain experience in videomaking, you can let your imaginations run amok, playing out some fantasies if you like. But in the beginning, I like to have couples simply record their acts of lovemaking by setting the camera, mounted on a tripod, to capture the scene. The setting doesn't matter, but since there will be no one else (we assume) to run the camera, you need to sort of "set it and forget it."

You're not trying for an Academy Award here, quite the contrary. You are going to make a very simple tape of you and your partner in the act of foreplay and intercourse. There won't be any closeups or planned dialogue. Your activity will be recorded by the camera. Later, you discuss what you see happening between the two of you. This "critique" of your lovemaking will give you insights into yourselves that you may not have known before.

You may see that you are saying or doing things to or with your partner that doesn't do a whole lot to advance the process of skill improvement. Couples often report that when they watched their first tape together, they were both able to see a particular point when they seemed to "shut down" with one another. Because they could see it themselves, they were able to talk about it and correct it.

In one case, where the female partner was still drinking and that awkward spot occurred in their lovemaking, she poured herself another drink and tried to just bluff it through. When the couple could watch their tape together, *sober,* and that same troublesome spot occurred, they could talk about ways to overcome the situation.

The troublesome spot was pretty obvious—oral sex. When I think of all the acts of sex and lovemaking that present itself as being difficult when sober, oral sex far and away holds first place. More couples complain to me that their sobriety halts or impairs the sharing of oral sex more than anything else they try to do. When a person is drinking, and the inhibitions are gone or short-circuited, then oral sex is not "dirty" or "messy" or "smelly."

When Janice and Carl were into their foreplay, Carl seemed to have a set routine, almost as if he were following a script. Janice sensed this routine and knowing that he was going to ask her to have oral sex, and knowing at just what spot that was going to occur in his "script," she began to tense up.

Oral sex had always been difficult for Janice to give; she loved it when Carl did it to her, but that was different somehow. When Janice was drinking, at the point in Carl's routine when she knew he was about to insist on her starting oral sex with him, she would bolster her courage by drinking. This enabled her to just "get through it." Watching their first videotape sober, both Janice and Carl picked up the fact that Carl's strict adherence to his routine "telegraphed" when that troublesome section was going to happen.

What was healing about the situation was that Carl recognized it first; he realized that he always said and did the same "old" things to Janice to start their foreplay. They laughed when watching the tape because it was Carl who suddenly blurted out to Janice, "Look out now, 'cause you're going to start giving head!"

Janice told me that she could feel herself getting tense as she played out his script and she had a very difficult time having oral sex without alcohol. Carl and Janice knew right away that one of the things they needed to do was find a way that she wouldn't be uptight about oral sex.

I suggested they vary the routine, not a little but a lot. Break the pattern of sameness, dissolve the barriers that Janice was setting up by fooling her as to when or even if that would even happen in their lovemaking. Carl wasn't too thrilled about the possibility that they wouldn't be having oral sex all the time, but agreed that he would make changes. Janice and Carl both agreed to the plan I proposed, which was to let Janice set the tone for once.

The Tape as a Turn-on

In viewing their next tape after they had agreed to this, Carl and Janice both felt as if they were watching two "very different people."

"We really got turned on watching ourselves on tape, which led to the best sex we'd had in a long time!" Janice said.

"I think the spontaneity that was produced when we were watching ourselves was exactly what was needed," Carl added.

After you have made one or two "training tapes," then you can start to expand. Begin by playing out one or the other's fantasy. I suggest to couples that they take turns from time to time in being the "director." If she is directing the sequence, then he must do what she has plotted out—no questions asked.

The exception to this, of course, is if either party feels uncomfortable doing something in the script, or isn't enjoying what the script is calling for.

If it is his turn to be the director, then she complies with his "script." You will find it very interesting to see how the simplest things, lit by candles and accompanied by music, can make a most artful and fun tape for you both. Go back to the basics; tape her getting ready and entering her bath, or tape the car/shower sequence that we dreamed up for the still picture project. You can set your camera in the kitchen and produce a tape of the two of you preparing a meal together. One important difference: As you are going through the dinner preparations, begin to remove articles of clothing from each other. I have suggested this scenario to many couples and they have reported back how stimulating the tape was for them both to make and to view later.

You can also choose a place in the woods or the mountains where videotaping one another or both of you together can be a delight and a far superior product to watch than two unknown professionals in some raunchy product carrying a triple "X" rating.

The more you try making your own video "productions," the more you can expand your skills as well as the scenarios you create. Our next and last project will further that design if you decide to tape your Character Roles.

CHARACTER ROLES

This should be, and is, a lot of fun for you and your partner. Here's the opportunity to act out your fantasies by assuming some of the different character roles that may have been a part of your fantasies. I have not put a "needed" list with this project, because I have no idea what your character roles might be.

Essentially, we are talking about costumes, masks, or makeup. Things that you have in your own wardrobe or things you might be willing to rent or buy to assume your character role, to enable you to act out your sexual fantasy to be someone else, or to be in another time and place.

As Alexandra Penny writes in *How to Make Love to a Man*, "We are just beginning to have the freedom to explore deeper levels of sexual fantasy; the world of the imagination may well be the next sexual frontier."

Assuming a character role might just be the thing to help you reach the new frontier of your relationship, and it's exciting and creative. What kind of character roles are chosen depends on your particular fantasies. Here are some basic ideas.

Fantasy Examples

Many women have sexual fantasies about being prostitutes or strippers. Many men fantasize about being masked in some form or another; such as a superhero from their comic book days.

Couples have told me of their playing "pirate" and "captured slave girl," or "cowboy" and "lady ranch owner," just to name two. One couple I worked with liked the idea of dressing as Japanese "geisha" and "feudal lord," and they took the pains and the time to obtain some old silken robes, sandals, and even some very inexpensive Halloween wigs that could be done up in "Japanese" hair styles. More than once they had a great experience by carrying out the whole scenario.

Another couple hit on the idea of an "Indian warrior" of some nameless tribe who captures and carries off a "dance hall girl," which allowed her to buy some new sexy garter belts, black net hose, and a teddy or two! He told me that he had some leather thong material, some tie ornaments and wooden beads, and threw on some "war paint" from makeup secured at a theatrical supply house. Neither outfit was very expensive and the female partner wanted the new lingerie anyhow.

I am confident that there are thousands of people who would like to be "Batman" or play the Julia Roberts role from *Pretty Woman*. What character you might assume, and what role you might choose to play, all depends on your sexual fantasy. So often, men's ideas of what women fantasize about are inaccurate. Women need to tell the men what turns them on and not vice versa!

However, it is very common (if you two have been reading the books I have suggested) for women to have some kind of fantasy about being "captured," "tied up," or some other form of not being in control of herself or the situation. Thus, character roles that allow for her "capture," roles that he can play to help her fantasy, are based on what the fantasy might be.

It isn't easy for anyone to reveal their fantasies. After all, they are secrets that remain locked in your mind until you conjure them up at *your* wish, not someone else's. If you have a difficult time in verbalizing your fantasy, simply get into the character role and then act it out. Your partner will quickly get the idea of what you use in sexual fantasy as a turn-on without you having to spell it out. The thing you must guard against is ever turning the fantasy *against* your partner after the lovemaking has ended.

It's Easy to be Vulnerable

In acting out fantasies, you both become very vulnerable; one of the reasons that character roles work so well is that you can act like someone else. This allows you to give your characters different names and makes it a safe thing to be able to refer to later, without causing hurt.

It's okay for the two of you to knowingly remark to one another that "Mazie, the dance hall girl really loves being stripped," whereas a remark addressed to your female partner by her real name and indicating that "I never knew you were such an exhibitionist!" is totally inappropriate. The person who makes such a remark begins to turn his or her partner's open sex play into a weapon to be used *against* the person.

Not only is this unfair, it works against the purpose of the exercise, which is to strengthen the relationship. When character roles can be easily assumed in foreplay, the sex acts themselves, and in the afterglow of lovemaking, they become wonderful vehicles to act out many of the "forbidden fruits" of your sexuality that you have perhaps had a hard time doing as your "normal" self.

Another plus for the project of Character Roles is that it allows you to let go of inhibitions for which you previously needed alcohol and/or other drugs in order to do. You may think that you could never get yourself into some kind of uniform or costume to play sex games, but once you have tried it, you will find that it becomes easier for you to play a role. You can relax and not be tense; no drink is necessary to loosen up to play the character you are in your sex game.

Some Danger Signs

There are some pitfalls you should be aware of. I remember a couple who were going to try the Character Role project. The woman dragged out their daughter's old cheerleader outfit, which her own well-turned figure could fill beautifully. She requested that he dress as a college professor. She had never graduated from college; pregnancy forced her to drop out.

She said that she had always fantasized about being selected as a cheerleader, and that she imagined herself rushing late into class and taking her seat in the front row, where her professor "couldn't keep his eyes off her in her short skirt." Her fantasy always had her being seduced by the professor, and she had used this imagery many times in her masturbation, always changing the scenarios but never the characters of the cheerleader and the professor.

Unfortunately, when this fantasy was played out, it was almost a disaster. With their son and daughter grown and gone to other cities, the wife had returned to school to complete her degree. Her husband became quite jealous of her references to her economics professor. The woman had no idea that her husband was harboring this jealousy, because he hadn't said anything. One of the reasons they were in therapy in the first place was to improve their poor communications, and his not sharing such feelings was pretty much the norm. Her fantasy of the cheerleader was a genuine one from her interrupted college days.

It was her husband who connected his own jealousy to the present-day situation and their attempt at strengthening their relationship backfired when he confronted her after their Character Role playing about her "desire and lust" for her real professor. She was totally stunned, since for her the whole thing was a reenactment of her fantasy, not an acting out of the present-day real-life situation. By discussing Character Roles and fantasies you can avoid the Character Roles being turned against you.

It Takes Effort and Planning

I am a great believer in the Character Role project because it requires effort and planning. That means you are giving real attention to the nurturing of your relationship. Nurture the relationship and there will be a sexual payoff. Besides, it's fun! You'd be surprised at what five dollars will buy in a Goodwill shop that you can use for your costuming.

Rummage around in your closets, the attic, the garage. Think of what your fantasy requires, and then do your best to obtain these things. The beauty of Character Roles for use in the Home Video Production ought to be obvious. What great fun you can have in just setting up your camera and playing out your fantasy embellished with some costumes, some makeup, and amateur acting.

You will get plenty of ideas from reading the material I have suggested. You will probably be amazed that so many others around the world have similar fantasies; you are definitely not alone.

The six "projects" involved in this chapter are games, so they should be taken in the spirit in which they have been devised. Think of them as games of love between you and your partner. When you do this you will have the spirit of what rebuilding a satisfying, stimulating, and highly satisfactory sex life can be in sobriety.

When so many couples seem to lose interest in each other because they can no longer be "drinking buddies" or "doping partners," it's sad. That doesn't ever have to happen to you! Remember, you had a certain fear about trying sexual things before, or you may have always wanted to do some things but didn't. Without alcohol to bolster you, you gave away the power over your sex life, believing that maybe things will "never be the same."

That simply is *not* true. You are the same person you were before the alcohol or drugs entered the picture. What you need to do is to let go of how things were and look at how things can be between you. Using the six projects—any or all of them—will absolutely pick up the pace in your sexual life and help you overcome the idea that without alcohol you can't "perform" or "enjoy" the sexuality that is your God-given gift.

Ten

Sober Sex for Gays and Lesbians

Through the years that my former partner Paul Staley and I owned and operated Gateway Treatment Center, we were privileged to have many gay and lesbian clients go through our program. I say privileged because I know of no more dedicated people in treatment; those we treated worked harder at getting and maintaining sobriety than the heterosexuals we saw.

Yet sobriety holds a much more fearful future for the homosexual man or woman than it does for heterosexuals, and the reasons for this are many. However, my experience indicates that sobriety, and particularly sex in the sober state, often moves right into the number one position of problem areas for the gay and lesbian couple.

FEELING VULNERABLE

In general terms, the gay or lesbian person is already dealing with fears and anxieties in specific areas: "coming-out" issues, general relationship problems that any couple has, identity issues, and self-acceptance problems. Self-love and the entire area of self-esteem are riddled with doubts, anxieties, and fears for the future, and of course, these are some of the reasons that the use of alcohol and/or other drugs have been used to help the gay or lesbian person deal with those fears.

When you stop to think about your own life, imagine what it would be like if you have been uncomfortable or uneasy with your life-style and have been drinking or drugging just to maintain that life-style. Now, being sober and being free from drug usage has taken that extra shield of safety from you; you feel naked, exposed, scared, and, believe me, *plenty* vulnerable. Dr. Gary Forrest sheds a bright light on a very dark corner of understanding about the homosexual alcoholic when he says, "Like the chronic alcoholic, some addictive homosexuals 'hit bottom' several times before they seek out help and begin the recovery process."

Dr. Forrest then puts the cap on the problem with, "For many people, alcohol addiction or alcohol abuse in combination with homosexuality precipitates involvement in a self-destructive trap, which all too often proves fatal."

OTHER PRESSURE AREAS

Homosexual men or women have other pressures besides the involvement in the relationship itself. Gay men still tend to be viewed as perverts, and they are feared more than ever as disease carriers, particularly as AIDS continues to sweep around the world.

Women, in large part due to the sexual liberation of the sixties, have shed some of the stigma of being gay, but they still pay a large emotional price because society regards same-sex living as "dirty," "perverted," "inappropriate," and other generic labels that substitute for ignorance. When Masters and Johnson wrote in 1979 that one in four adult males in this country has experienced overt homosexual behavior, people expressed shock.

Masters and Johnson opened the "secret door" of homosexual behavior even farther when they reported that men and women fantasize and *think* about homosexual activities on a pretty regular basis, and of course Nancy Friday's works on women's sexual fantasies indicate a far larger number of women have same-sex fantasies *and* actual lesbian experiences than expected.

THE ROLE OF ALCOHOL AND DRUGS

It is absolutely safe to say that most of these experiences, whether repeated or not, were greatly influenced by the use of alcohol or other drugs, usually marijuana and cocaine.

It would be pure "ostrich-like behavior" to think that if you took away the alcohol or drugs that enabled a person to have a same-sex sexual experience that homosexual behavior would just naturally continue. It might, and it often does, but more often than not, women and men who use alcohol or drugs to have same-gender sex believe they need the alcohol and drugs to do it again.

Remember, drugs short circuit inhibitions that might keep one from experimenting with gay or lesbian sex.

Therefore, without the very chemicals that have helped make it possible for hidden homosexual thoughts to become *overt* behavior, fear, anxiety, and doubt almost certainly reappear.

THE SEXUAL APPETITE DWINDLES

The homosexual man or woman may very well be trying to handle a double-edge sword at a time in his or her life that he or she needs the most security: the period of early sobriety.

I have found, in my practice with gay men and women, that it is not uncommon for their sexual appetite to drop off considerably at the onset of sobriety; not because they could not perform but because they began to question the very essence of their homosexuality in the first place. Simply put, if a man or woman was hesitant about "coming-out" in the first place and the use of alcohol or some other drug helped make that decision easier, then when the brakes of sobriety are applied, that same man or woman may suddenly pause and say, "Is this life-style really for me?"

If a person is bisexual, they seem able to practice this behavior as long as they are drinking or drugging. They seem quite comfortable and content to have sex with either a man or a woman, sometimes carrying on multiple affairs at the same time. Many times, the other partners will be unaware of this dual sexual behavior.

However, when a bisexual person enters sobriety, many times it tends to focus the person toward one sexual identity or another, not both.

CONFUSION LEADS TO RELAPSE

Transvestism, "cross dressing," mild cases of s/m behavior can all be practiced and nourished rather exuberantly when the participants are pretty well oiled on booze or high on pot or cocaine.

If, however, absolute sobriety and "straight" (nondrug use) behavior is being practiced, is dressing up in panties, bra, and a garter belt as easy? Here it is evident that the man who is struggling with his gender identity may not continue along the path he has been living when he undertook sobriety, and if the pain of giving up that part of his sexuality is too great, you can just about count on a relapse.

It becomes even more critical, then, for you to be helped along the path of comfortable gender identity as a boost to maintaining sobriety. More than one "straight" patient has relapsed because they couldn't handle the prospect of sexual failure, or felt the pressure of performance to be so great as to lead them back into the bottle.

SOBRIETY CAN BE A THREAT

If the commitment for the gay man or woman in a homosexual relationship is "iffy" to begin with, if one of the parties is already questioning the relationship, then entering sobriety might be just the push that is needed to end the relationship. It's no different from a heterosexual relationship. This is particularly true if alcohol was a really big factor in the dating process to begin with.

As we've continued to stress in this book, most of your sexual experiences have involved alcohol from the very beginning, so it's quite likely that when alcohol is taken out of the relationship, then the relationship is not going to be the same. If you are gay or lesbian, if you have struggled with the identity question in the first place, then the sobriety is really going to point up the struggle you may be feeling.

YOUR COMFORT LEVEL

Without even addressing the sobriety question, it is imperative that you look at how comfortable you are in the lifestyle you are living. Are you openly maintaining a homosexual relationship? Do your friends and relatives know of your relationship? Have your friends and relatives accepted this relationship?

Any of these questions could probably bring out pages of material for discussion. However, if you have hidden your relationship, you have really hidden *yourself*. This real you, the one that everyone thinks they know, is not there at all. You are, or have been, living a lie, and the path of sobriety will only make that lie more obvious to you.

I remember a patient of mine who was one of the most talented men I had known. A professional himself, he struggled with that "double-edged" sword of which I spoke earlier. Not only did his family not know about his alcoholism, but they didn't have a clue about his gay relationship — a relationship of almost twenty years' duration. The pressure to decide which issue to disclose to his family kept this man in a constant state of turmoil.

He relapsed consistently after visits home, torn in anguish with having to live the *two* enormous lies that comprised the majority of his adult life. He was not to be free of this pain until his therapy helped him to make the choice to disclose.

My patient chose to own up to the alcoholism first. He received unanimous support for his recovery, which gradually allowed him to disclose his homosexuality to family members, one at a time. While it was a long and slow process, the patient nevertheless understood the task, knowing that his parents' deeply religious background was going to be brutally assaulted by his disclosure.

I had pressed him for a decision to disclose and his anger at me was evident; I was becoming the enemy and no longer in support of him and his recovery.

We kept at it until the therapy brought him to a comfort level about himself that allowed him to take the action of disclosure.

"Are you happy being gay?" I would ask.

"You damn well know I can't be any other way!" he would snap back.

"Then what is keeping you from disclosing the real you?" I would ask.

"It would kill my parents to know that I was gay!" he fairly screamed at me.

"Did it kill them to know you're an alcoholic?" I asked. "Are they not being incredibly supportive of you in treatment?" And finally I asked, "What makes you think they will stop loving you as a son, a homosexual son, any more than they stopped loving you as an alcoholic son?"

"But it's *different*!" he lamented. "They can *handle* me being an alcoholic."

"And I tell you, particularly after twenty years of being in a gay relationship, they will also handle you being gay," I said. "And if they don't, will you *stop* being gay and return to a heterosexual life?"

"Of course not," he replied. "I'm only comfortable being gay; I've *never* been comfortable when I had to pretend at dating women."

You see, this patient had to arrive at stating his comfort level; he had to reinforce for himself, that his gay life-style was where he wanted to be no matter the consequences of disclosure. He did it. He started with the sister he had been closest to, and she was openly supportive and loving to him. That gave him the courage to tackle his other siblings. As I had suspected, they all knew anyway, but the family was widely scattered about the country and so the matter had never been brought up and discussed among them.

GAINING CONFIDENCE IN WHO YOU ARE

As my patient became more reinforced by his brothers and sisters, it became evident that he was more and more comfortable with who he was, and therefore, when it came time to tell his parents, it went smooth as silk. Since he wasn't apologizing for his life-style, he had confidence in the way he decided to present his case to his parents.

His mom and dad were pretty judgmental at first, doing all the blaming and questioning that many parents of gays and lesbians unfortunately posture around. Then he simply gave them an option that we had discussed in therapy. They could disown him, but needed to make it clear that they were accepting him as an alcoholic and rejecting him as a homosexual, or they could accept the fact that he was working on the destructive part of his life, the alcoholism, which was helping him build the most productive and worthwhile part of his life, the relationship that was more solid than any of the marriages of his siblings, none of whom had been with the same mate for the same twenty-year period he had been in his relationship.

Happily, the parents unruffled their own feathers, stopped blaming themselves because he hadn't "turned out right," and gained a comfort level of their own in which to relate to their son. He has not relapsed for many months, and his prognosis to graduate from treatment is excellent. His life of sobriety seems well ordered now, and his relationship with his partner has grown even more solid.

When my patient secured his comfort level, he and his partner's sex life not only resumed but increased in frequency and partner participation to a level of mutual satisfaction.

MISTAKEN RELATIONSHIP PROBLEM

While drinking, Tanya and Carol's relationship seemed ideal, but after only a few weeks of sobriety, Tanya became surly, difficult, and withdrawn from her partner.

Sex came to an abrupt and door-slamming halt. Carol was confused, angry, hurt, and outright incensed by Tanya's behavior.

"Goddammit, when you were drinking, we never had these problems!" Carol yelled at Tanya in my office during joint therapy. But Tanya shot back angrily.

"Oh, we *had* them all right! I just *ignored* them because I was drinking!"

Unfortunately they were both right. There was no question here of the comfort area of lesbianism — that was not the issue at all, nor had it been for either woman for many years. The *real* issue was the fact that sobriety had suddenly thrown its harsh beam on Tanya's understanding that she was in the wrong relationship, period.

Carol was not a neat person; she did not keep her clothes or possessions in any kind of order, and Tanya was just this side of being a first-class "neat freak." The "visual pollution" as Tanya put it, was driving her crazy. Carol had tried several times to do things around the house the way Tanya wanted them done, but facing it honestly, neatness had very little priority in Carol's life.

Carol was an artist, a sculptress and painter, and the rooms of their house reflected Carol's occupation and her talent. Tanya had met and fallen in love with Carol at an exhibition of Carol's work in a small downtown gallery.

When they got together, Tanya overlooked the piles of materials, drop cloths, paints, brushes, clays, and so on that seemed to be occupying every nook and cranny of Carol's home—into which Tanya had moved.

SOBRIETY LEADING TO RESENTMENT

Tanya was a teacher; to her, order, organization, and "being in charge" were paramount credos for living an enriched life. Alcohol was also a priority in her life, and Tanya was clearly drinking alcoholically. While drinking, Tanya overlooked the "visual pollution" that sobriety suddenly brought into sharp focus. When she was in her drinking stage, Tanya's complaints were quickly soothed over in the passion of the love-making that she and Carol shared, and a sort of "to hell with it" attitude pervaded the relationship.

But with the onset of sobriety, all of Tanya's pent-up resentment at the way Carol was living—indeed, the way Carol was forcing Tanya to live—came to a head and erupted. Here was one of those cases when I felt sure Carol was going to turn into a first-class saboteur of treatment. She was fearful of losing her relationship with Tanya, something that had not been in jeopardy while Tanya was drinking.

However, an intervention by Tanya's principal had sent Tanya and Carol into alcohol treatment at our Gateway Treatment Center, and now, some months later, Tanya was threatening to leave the relationship. It had become clear in therapy that Tanya was feeling more and more that she was in the wrong relationship to begin with, that she had entered it in awe of Carol's talent and, as the weeks and months had slipped by, simply ignored through drink, the messy way of life she was living.

With sobriety, her resolve not to have to live in a constant state of disarray became firm. She was convinced that what she had taken as love for Carol was really just heroine worship, and that ultimately, Carol would never change. Carol, for her part, was terribly committed to making the relationship work; she *would* change, she *could* become the "neat freak" Tanya seemed to want.

SOBER REALIZATIONS

But it was not to be. The more Carol tried to be what Tanya wanted, the more her work suffered. She was spending more time on cleaning, arranging, and sorting and stacking materials and things of her craft than she was on the creative process. Sex had stopped between them and the one or two attempts that Carol made to reinstate it were dismal failures. Tanya realized more and more that she was in the wrong place with the wrong person.

To her credit, Tanya saw that Carol's creative work was suffering because she was putting her energies into making the changes that weren't really comfortable for her at all. Had Tanya been weaker, I'm sure she would have returned to drinking and continued to slip farther and farther back into the abyss, stuffing her resentment at the way they lived but allowing the alcohol to medicate her anger.

Instead, Tanya left the relationship, convinced it had been wrong from the beginning; she needed to be out of it to be healthy. Staying was destructive for them both. Realizing her "mistaken relationship" cleared the path for Tanya to make important, healthy changes in her life. Carol soon became involved with a woman who lived her same "loose" style, thus removing the pressure from her life to be something she was not.

BUILDING A NEW BRIDGE IN A HOMOSEXUAL RELATIONSHIP

It's very evident that gay and lesbian relationships require new bridge-building just as heterosexual relationships do.

However, if you *are* gay or lesbian there are some myths about yourselves and your sexuality that may have victimized you, prevented you from taking some of the steps to the new bridge-building that sobriety requires. For example:

The level of sexual interest is the *same* between homosexuals and heterosexuals. If you are very active sexually, there is nothing "wrong" with you. Gays have no more or less sexual activity than their hetero counterparts.

This includes the widely held belief that if you are black you engage in more sex than if you are white. Statistically this is not true. Also untrue is the belief that gay sexual activity is greater among men than women, or that younger gays engage in more sexual activity than older ones.

Some of the things about your sexual life-style that *are* true, however, may be of help to you along the sober sex route.

If you are gay you *do* have more sexual contacts, as far as numbers go, than heterosexuals, with gay men having more sexual contacts than gay women.

If you are a lesbian, you treat relationships in the same manner as your heterosexual sisters—that is, there is very little straying outside the relationship. That's good news for you, since sobriety will probably make you seem less adventuresome anyhow, most of the "bottle courage" disappearing with your recovery.

Relationships among gay men tend to be more open than among lesbians. Gay men tend to put up with a lot of flirting behavior from their partner. This is no myth. Researchers have found that 20–35 percent of the gay population are chemically dependent, so you are not alone if you have had a drug or alcohol problem and are also gay or lesbian. The key to your sexual success in sobriety is to be able and willing to take the same element of risk that the heterosexual must take to *make changes* in your life.

BEING DIFFERENT ISN'T EASY

Indeed, it's not easy being different, and the gay and lesbian couples who have "come out" and attempted to build lives within their communities have found themselves facing enormous pressures. Society still has a difficult time accepting a different sexual life-style and preference than what has always been the "norm," but add to that the burden of recovering from alcoholism, and the stimga for the gay or lesbian is almost unbearable.

I say this with such certainty because of all the times I have set in my office with a gay or lesbian couple and listened to one of them say: "It's bad enough that I'm gay; God help me that I'm also alcoholic!"

And the confusion continues to reign in the mind of that person and his or her significant other. There is a fear inherent in disclosing alcoholism, but to have to disclose both alcoholism and homosexuality becomes a burden that is easy to talk about but difficult to share.

A NEW ELEMENT

A person may be alcoholic and gay but *recovering,* and that's just like throwing an entirely new third person into the relationship. Everything that seemed to be working in the relationship when you were drinking no longer works. There are new ground rules, new behaviors emerging, and certainly new demands that the gay and lesbian lover places upon his or her partner in sobriety. What seemed to be okay when drinking or drugging, what seemed to be sexually stimulating, satisfying, and rewarding no longer seems to be any of those things and the couple sits around and wonders, "What's wrong, anyhow?"

Quite simply, you are *not* the same person you were when you were drinking, so it stands to reason that a new set of guidelines needs to be in place for you to operate within your relationship.

HONEST SEX

This isn't a subject that applies only to the gay/lesbian couple; it's appropriate for *everyone* who engages in sex.

But what we want to do is answer some perplexing questions:

> What do I like?
> What don't I like?
> How about frequency?
> Who needs to be the initiator?

When you were drinking, the act of sex itself was initiated and consummated without a whole lot of thought. Promiscuity is rampant when one is drinking, and very little serious thought is ever put into making sure that both partner's needs are being met. Sex with anyone who is drinking is pretty much a "rough and tumble" moment or two of what I call "feeley-grabby," and in some cases there may be genuine satisfaction—orgasm, loving, caring, tenderness. But mostly, if you will be totally honest, not a whole lot of time was spent in finding out or discussing what you really liked in the way of sex. There was too much attention paid to not letting the moments of passion pass without being answered—passion, I might add, that was mostly fueled by alcohol.

You must now sit down with your partner and ask some tough questions of each other centered around whether your needs are being met sexually. By that I mean whether what are you doing sexually is really what "rings your chimes." It may be just dandy with your partner, but not really sit well with you at all. Sobriety is making it possible for "honesty" to be a part of your mental and physical vocabulary. Your partner may not be ready to hear "honesty." He or she has been under the impression that what you were both doing sexually was just fine, and now here you are telling him or her that certain parts of your lovemaking were *not* okay, and furthermore, you want to change them. Well, that's going to be a bitter pill for your partner to swallow, and very possibly it will be met with many "Why's."

Forget the "Why" and concentrate on the "How" (do we make changes), "When" (do we get started?), and "What" (do we do) to make it all happen. If everything you did when drinking is still okay, then don't change anything. In this case just reaffirm that "I really like when you do such and such." This will help reinforce for you and your partner that your sex life is growing and nourishing both of you. But if, as I know is the case more times than not, there are one or two things that you not only dislike but actually *hate*, then you will never be able to fake it again now that you are sober. Exercising gentleness and understanding for your partner's feelings ensures that he or she understands it isn't something that they are doing differently but rather something that you never really cared for in the first place. Now you want his or her help in replacing that event with one that will work better for both of you.

A typical example is a couple wherein one partner always wants to watch a porno film before having sex. The other partner has always hated this but felt obligated to participate. The reluctant watcher always felt as if the lover was getting turned on by the film and just using the partner to relieve the sexual tension. "It wasn't more than mutual masturbation," the patient told me.

Addressing the question of "What do I like/dislike?" involves some risk, but remember that is what getting well is all about—taking risks, making changes.

When you come to the questions that surround frequency and instigation of sex, the same parameters must be in place. You are not complaining about how things have been in the past, merely suggesting that in your sobriety it's time to look at some areas of discomfort or displeasure in your past sexual activities.

Drinking may have cast you in the role of always being the aggressor, always being the one who needed to "make the moves" if there was to be any sex. Maybe that's how it had all started between you in the first place, and there has never been any reason to change. But now you must clearly examine whether these roles have been comfortable for you. What's it like to always be the one to instigate sex? What's it like to know that the frequency of your sexual encounters may have been decreed by the meeting of your partner's needs with little or no consideration for your own?

I am constantly amazed at the patients who complain to me about the "infrequent" sex that takes place in their home. When I press them for numbers I find that many of them are complaining because they *only* have sex five times a week instead of every day. Or they complain because they *only* have sex *once* a day. This is far from the norm; sex occurring once a week is the national average.

It's important to stop looking at and living up to quotas and get on with looking at what works for your relationship.

CHANGING SEX ROLES

Like all activities that deal with human sexual behavior, it's easy to let confusion reign. How many times has it been professed that men were looking for a woman who "could be a whore in the bedroom, but a lady in the kitchen"? Cross dressing is a manner of behavior that allows escape from the given biologic role assigned to one's life; it's a fantasy role that can be played and embellished with the addition or subtraction of articles of clothing. In your relationship, however, a deeper confusion of roles may exist. You may have been "passive" or the "receiver" of sex in your relationship, particularly when drinking.

Now that you are sober, ask yourself, "Am I comfortable in this role?" and "Do I *always* want to be the one who receives love and passion and never gives?" You may also question whether you want to be the aggressor—and this is not to be confused with the role of instigator of sex.

In gay relationships, for example, are you content to play the traditional feminine and perhaps more passive role? Is this role different from your normal behavior when you are both out in public?

I treated a couple who had complete role reversals in and out of their bedroom. To the outside world, Keith was dominant; he made all the financial decisions for himself and Steven. The house had been selected and the down payment made by Keith; the furniture and their cars all bore the imprint of Keith's strong, affirmative, and controlling hand. He was also the alcoholic in the relationship. In the bedroom, the roles were totally reversed. Keith relinquished all decisions regarding love, sex, and romance in general. He wanted to be the passive, more "female" of the two.

Of course, things changed one they came into treatment. As Keith began his sobriety, he discovered that the aggressive role he maintained for the outside world but gave up in the bedroom was too much of a dichotomy in his life. He wanted to continue in his "male" role while they were instigating and engaging in their sexual life.

This left Steven hurt, angry, and confused over what he considered the best part of their relationship. Many hours of individual therapy and then joint therapy were needed to resolve that it was "okay" to change roles within their relationship and not have either of them feel threatened with the loss of power.

It became okay for Keith to be the dominant lover every so often, and as a matter of fact, Steven became rather fond of being pampered and looked after in his new role as the passive member of the relationship. They became comfortable in switching roles; it added to the spice of their sex life as well as fostered some fantasy material that both had often talked about but never carried out. Without sobriety, the issue would never have been addressed, but once it was, it became a wonderful challenge for both Keith and Steven to see how best the other's needs could be more enriched, thus enriching their own.

The idea is to be able to face the fact that the roles you and your partner are playing "outside"—that is, in real life— are not necessarily the roles that you need or want to continue on the "inside"—your bedroom. It's okay to make a change.

EXPANDING THE RELATIONSHIP
WITHOUT JEALOUSY

How do you feel about:

Going places besides "gay bars"?
Being open and affectionate to others?
Having heterosexual friends who don't drink?
Going places without your partner?
Taking time out for yourself?

The answers to these questions represent your ability to
expand your relationship without the jealousy that normally
accompanies such moves. You may be surprised to realize
how many times you turned to the bottle to overcome your
feelings about just these issues. Any one may have lead you
to a drink so you could either participate in them or coun-
teract your jealous feelings when your partner did them.

But now, in sobriety, you need to expand your own life
in order to be able to enrich the relationship between the two
of you. Imagine a love relationship where neither partner
ever saw a movie without the other one, or never met new
and interesting people, or talked world affairs, war, football,
the ballet or theater with no one except the person with
whom they are involved.

It would be an incredibly dull and boring relationship,
and yet thousands and thousands of couples live that way.
You need to break away from the mold of sameness. Your
sex life will be greatly enhanced by your expanding world —
and I certainly don't mean that you should have sexual encounters with a variety of partners! I mean that you continue
to bring new, fresh, and invigorating ideas, opinions, and
color to your relationship when you begin to meet your own
socialization needs.

EXPANDING YOUR LIFE

For a long time, everything you may have done involved
other gays; you went only to gay bars, never went out with-

out your partner for fear he or she would "find someone else." Well, the AIDS epidemic, which makes monogamy almost a mandate, should help relieve your anxiety about the casual "one-night stand" of yore, so maybe you can expand your social world without fear of losing your partner.

Fresh ideas, thoughts, and viewpoints all come from doing some things that enhance your world away from that of your partner. Sobriety can allow you to do that now, so you might return from the theater or a movie with much to discuss with your partner, who perhaps was unable to accompany you. How secure would you be in suggesting that your partner go somewhere without *you?* Would it be okay for him or her to renew friendships with old friends even if you were not along to "guard" the relationship?

A true mark of your sobriety will be to rebuild the elements of trust between you and your partner. Are you going to come all "unglued" if your partner showed affection to someone else while in your company? The growth of your sexual life is at stake here, for the old adage of "If you love someone let him go, and if he comes back to you he is yours" applies. The rest of that adage also applies: "If he *doesn't* come back, then he never was yours."

When you were drinking or drugging, jealousy controlled your relationship. So now, in sobriety, you can see the strength of the love you and your partner share by allowing that person some freedom to build the kind of nurturing *they* need in order to continue to nurture *your* relationship.

If you never allow someone to take care of themselves, how can they possibly have the energy, the strength, or the desire to help take care of your relationship?

The alcohol and the drugs kept you tethered to each other; that doesn't have to be the case anymore, and the more you practice being your own person the more your relationship can grow. Trust builds trust, faith nurtures more faith, and your gay or lesbian partner needs the freedom to breathe the air of their own life to better bring more energy into the relationship with you!

Again, gay and lesbian couples often feel more threatened by allowing their partner this kind of freedom than straight couples do. Straight couples get in just as much of a jealousy bind as gay couples, but the threat to the relationship is not nearly as strong.

I have known gay and lesbian couples who were absolutely miserable at an activity or family gathering but were so insecure in the relationship that they forced themselves to go, just so they could "keep an eye on" their partner. And of course the alcohol that may have been consumed at these events didn't help the trust level much either.

All that can change and for the better! Your partner needs to be let off the leash and given the trust that he or she deserves. Your sex life will reap the rewards far more than you imagine if you allow your partner the freedom he or she deserves, without the jealousy that marked your relationship in the past. You do not need a drink because your partner is going to see an old high school chum without you.

He or she is not going to fall into bed with the old friend, even though you may fight those monsters in your head for a while. I tell my patients to "trust the process" and that's what I say to you, too. The process is sobriety and the new ways to allow your relationship with your gay or lesbian partner to expand and grow without stifling or controlling it.

The rewards for this kind of new behavior will show up in the bedroom (or on the couch in front of the TV!) if you will just put some of this relaxation into practice. You need to *allow* it for your partner; you need to *practice* it for yourself.

CHANGING ROLES IN PARENTING

Changes occur when the gay or lesbian couple introduces a possible switch in parenting. Suppose your child is living with you and your lover. Maybe, while drinking, the parenting chores, for the most part, fell to your lover because it "interfered" in some way with your drinking life-style. Naturally, there was bonding between her and your child. In sobriety, you want to go back to being a mother.

How hard will it be for your lover to suddenly return the reins of parenting over to you? How hard will it be on the child? Whose needs are best being served by making such a drastic role switch? These are very tough questions, and they need a great deal of discussion between all of you in order to arrive at what's best for all concerned. My point is, those are all difficult role change potentials, and there will be many hours of sharing and giving and taking for you to arrive at workable solutions.

But arrive you must for the road to your sobriety may indeed have suddenly taken you down the one marked "parenting" in such a strong fashion that you will be surprised at its force.

I recall a lesbian couple who had four children living with them—three of one partner and one of the other. When the partner with the three children was drinking and drinking heavily, almost all of the parenting in the household fell to her lover.

When sobriety struck, that household erupted in an incredible explosion of temper, of threats, and of general chaos. The woman who had been the drinker was suddenly back in the role of mother that she had not only neglected but for which she was pretty inept and unprepared. Her husband had left her for another woman; she had turned to alcohol to numb that pain and discovered her own lesbian feelings.

She and her children moved in with her lesbian lover who was an excellent and loving mother to her own nine-year-old daughter.

Giving Up Parenting

The drinking mother was only too happy to have her lover be the major caregiver to all the children. But when the drinking reached the crisis stage, as it inevitably does, and an intervention took place, recovery brought about an icy-cold realization that she was still a single mother with the ultimate responsibility for raising her three children.

It was a very frightening experience for this woman, I assure you, but with the love and help of her therapy support group, her A.A. group, and her partner, not to mention *all* the children, this lady fought back and is still fighting for her rightful role in her children's lives.

Sobriety has been hard for her because it caused the realization of her lack of parenting skills, but she is sticking with it.

Letting Go Is Hard

Her lover has had to change, too. She needed to turn the parental reins back over to the rightful mother and thus "let go" of some strong attachments she had made to her partner's children.

For a time, the women were strangers to each other, sleeping in separate beds, in separate rooms, both unable to bridge the gap that had grown between them. The pressure upon the two women caused a cessation of their sexual life. They even considered separating and ending the relationship, but another lesbian couple, who had experienced and survived much the same trauma in their relationship, had strongly recommended counseling.

When they finally worked through the issue of parenting skills — or rather the lack of parenting skills — with their therapist and in their group, sex started again, better than ever, for now they had formed a new bond of understanding, compassion, and a willingness to learn and share that their former situation, besotted with the one's alcoholism, failed to deliver.

The children did a kid's group at the treatment center with great success, and it is evident as you see this couple and their kids today, how far they have come. It was incredibly difficult, but this couple was committed to making the changes that would make their relationship stronger, more durable, and more rewarding for all of them.

If you are homosexual, sobriety will offer many challenges and will taunt you just as the realization and acknowledgment of your sexuality did. You are entitled to have, to share, to be a part of a wonderful and fulfilling sexual adventure with that special person in your life.

For every fear you have had that you have drowned in another swallow of alcohol, there is a ray of hope in sobriety. You no longer need to use alcohol to "excuse" your sexual preferences, or to make them acceptable even to yourself, much less others. Sex and sobriety are yours in an entirely new and different way if you will reach out and not be afraid to link them with the same persistence and dedication that you link your love and your life to another of your sex.

Eleven

Sex and AIDS

In 1991 the Center for Disease Control (CDC) told the nation that every ten minutes another American was dying of AIDS (Acquired Immune Deficiency Syndrome). Fred Hellinger, the director for the division of cost and financing at the federal agency for Health Care Policy and Research, also told the country that AIDS treatment was going to cost a hefty $5.8 billion for the year 1991.

Hellinger breaks this monstrous figure down to a cost of annual treatment for one AIDS patient at $32,000. The treatment of HIV (Human Immunodeficiency Virus) infection was estimated to cost $1.4 billion, and that's for people diagnosed HIV positive but who did not yet have AIDS. Hellinger said that the average annual cost to treat HIV positive patients in 1991 was going to run $5,100 per patient.

So far, we've just looked at the enormous dollar costs of the AIDS epidemic. The emotional cost to the nation is incalculable.

THE IMPACT OF "MAGIC"

Late in 1991 the world was shocked to hear basketball star Magic Johnson announce that he was HIV positive. A few days later, Johnson reaffirmed his statement and said that he had acquired the problem from heterosexual encounters prior to his marriage.

Suddenly, it seemed, this disease was real. It wasn't just the "gay men's disease" that had held so much of the world's attention. Johnson brought the problem squarely home to the millions of "straight" men and women. He was proof that people can and do contract the deadly virus through heterosexual activity—a fact that had been stated from the very beginning of the epidemic but little believed.

THE GROWING NUMBERS

AIDS is a tragedy that we must face squarely; there is no longer a way to run down the complicated and busy streets of modern life and ignore the enemy that is lurking, ready to strike, to kill. First identified in 1981, AIDS as a disease has achieved epidemic proportions and the figures are constantly changing.

In 1981 there were 376 reported AIDS cases in the United States. In 1990 there were 146,746, and by the year 1993 the projected number of reported AIDS cases is 450,000. For every person who has AIDS, there are seven to ten people who are HIV positive—that is, people who are infected and infectious.

Unless there is a dramatic medical breakthrough or cure for AIDS, we are dealing with an epidemic in every sense of the word. This is something that gets worse, not better.

COUNTING HIV

In 1991 the World Health Organization estimated that by the end of the decade, *40 million* people will be infected with HIV and at least 10 million diagnosed with AIDS. We have

seen a slowing of the disease in the United States, largely due
to the change in sex behavior of some groups such as gays.
But, these changes have overshadowed the "accelerated rates
of HIV infection in other groups, such as women and people
of color," says Elizabeth Korineck, M.P.H., writing in *AIDS
Newslink.*

To date, slightly more than 10 percent of those infected
with HIV in the United States have developed AIDS.

IMPORTANCE TO THE DRINKING AND DRUGGING PERSON

The importance to the alcoholic or the drug abuser is pro-
found. When you were drinking or under the influence of
other drugs, how much did you know about your sex partners? Did you ever *think* about using condoms or not sharing
"works" (needles, syringes)?

Alcohol-induced black-outs barely let you remember who
was waking up in bed beside you, so how many really important details of your past sexual encounters do you remember? An honest evaluation of this behavior is essential if
you are to see the link between sex, drink, and drugs. We
know that there is a very strong connection between substance abuse and AIDS.

Some people have exchanged sex for money or drugs,
which increases their vulnerability to contract HIV. When
you were drinking or using you were probably also having
more sex; you were experiencing what we call "hypersexu-
ality," a state of activity that gave you the opportunities to
have sex indiscriminately and with a variety of partners,
doing many different things, and most often taking no precautions whatsoever.

THE SEXUAL REVOLUTION

In the sixties the concept of "if it feels good, do it!" led to a
freewheeling and much-talked-about sexual revolution

where all the "flower children," the "love goddesses," the "hippies" were co-habitating, partner swapping, engaging in "open marriage," and all the other acts of sexual freedom that seemed to burst upon the scene like a gigantic fireworks display.

It wasn't just the "flower children" and the "great un-washed masses," as some called them, who were enjoying this sexual revolution; it was crossing a very wide range of society, touching all walks of life.

Now, in the nineties, things have changed dramatically. No longer can one just go out there and partake of the one-night stands, the partner swapping, and the rest of it. There is a killer out there, and its name is AIDS.

IGNORANCE ABOUNDS

There is much ignorance about this disease. Somehow, the idea that this is a disease that "happens only to blacks and gays" has erected a barrier to the very knowledge that could save your life. Remember that *everyone* needs to practice safe sex. In fact, the only sure way not to get the AIDS virus is to be celibate, to abstain, something that probably isn't what you see for your life-style at all.

Just to point out how rapidly things have changed, can you remember just a few short months ago when the "buzz word" around town was the need to practice "safe" sex? Well that terminology is being replaced rapidly. The key word now is "safer" sex, clearly implying that as long as another person is involved in your sexual activity, you are at risk unless you take very strict precautions.

THE HIV VIRUS

First, let's look at the HIV virus itself and try to understand it better. As pointed out earlier, HIV stands for Human Immunodeficiency Virus. This virus is devastating because it attacks key cells in the immune system, cells that direct the body's response to disease. A person can become infected with HIV and have absolutely no observable symptoms either at the beginning or a decade later. In fact, some symptoms of HIV can be confused with other symptoms, such as those we see in withdrawal. Laboratory tests, two in particular, are necessary to help confirm the presence of the HIV virus. The two tests are the ELISA, which is an acronym for Enzyme-Linked Immunosorbent Assay, and Western Blot, a more specific and more expensive test that is generally used to confirm the results of a positive ELISA.

NO AIDS TEST

A point that should be stressed here is that you will often hear people refer to an "AIDS test," or "I've been tested for AIDS." Technically speaking there is no such thing as an "AIDS test." What a person is being tested for is the presence of the HIV virus. AIDS is the *end stage* of the HIV viral disease that impairs the body's ability to fight disease. HIV is an official designation, started in August 1986, to identify the virus that attacks the human system and usually leads to AIDS.

THE BODY HOSTS

There has to be a "host" for the transmission of the HIV virus—that is, a means by which it enters the human body. The most prominent of these hosts, in descending order, are:

Through the blood
Through semen
Through vaginal fluids
Through breast milk

The presence of two female-specific hosts points out that AIDS appears to hit women harder, and in fact, the HIV virus proceeds to the AIDS stage quicker in women. Even though the highest risk to contract HIV is through the blood, the most common method of transmission is through sex. And when we further break down sexual contact we find that the highest risk factors look like this:

Male to male
Male to female
Female to female

The last category is rare but it *does* occur.

Looking at human blood as a "host" to the HIV virus, the orders of highest risk are:

Sharing drug injection "works" (needles, syringes, cotton, cooker, or water)
Blood transfusions or hemophilia treatments
Unsterile instruments that puncture the skin such as in tattooing
Mishandling during blood-involved operations—call these "needle sticks"

Your risk factor is even higher depending on where you live. The list compiled by the Center for AIDS and Substance Abuse Training ranks the high-risk states as follows:

New York
California
Florida
Texas
New Jersey
Illinois
Puerto Rico
Pennsylvania
Georgia
Massachusetts

If you consider that 30 percent of the people who are HIV positive will develop AIDS within the first five years of becoming infected, then you can imagine the enormity of the epidemic.

DISPELLING RUMORS

So far we have talked about how you could get the HIV virus. Now, dispelling some wild rumors, here's how you *don't* get it: by using public toilets, swimming pools, elevators, buses, or by sharing eating and drinking utensils.

The HIV virus is not an airborne virus, so even if someone with HIV or someone who actually has AIDS shakes your hand, or sneezes on you, you won't get AIDS. This is a book about sex and sobriety so the number one thing to remember about this killer disease is that you have to practice safer sex, and that you definitely have to maintain your sobriety/recovery.

What do I mean by safer sex? What's okay?

KNOWING SEXUAL HISTORY

Admittedly, my focus in the preceding chapters has been on the potential that can be found in a committed, one-to-one relationship—that is, a relationship that is essentially monogamous, keeping yourselves on an "exclusively yours" sexual basis.

If you are not in a monogamous relationship, safer sex is a cardinal rule. In fact, even if you are in a committed relationship, unless you know the sexual history of your partner, unless the two of you have never had sex with an IV drug user, unless neither of you has had another partner or a bisexual or gay sexual experience in the last ten years, you could be at risk.

There's a truism among health-care professionals as we counsel our patients on this subject. "When you are sleeping with someone, you are also sleeping with *whoever they* slept with before they were with you."

You would think that knowledge about HIV would be

enough to make a person extra cautious; unfortunately, I meet many, many people of all ages who have long ago abandoned the idea of "having" to use condoms. "It's too damn much bother!" they say. Or, "I *know* this person and I *know* they don't have AIDS."

Well, you *don't* know, and that's why it's so important to continue practicing safer sex. While you may earnestly believe that your partner isn't HIV positive, you really don't know if he or she has been infected and the disease is just lying dormant, not yet breaking out into the system.

BEING HIV POSITIVE

HIV is transmitted through body fluids. It attacks and destroys specific cells in the body: T4 cells. At a 1990 workshop for professionals on AIDS, Fred Pottle of the Colorado State Department of Health and Jennifer Elpers, LCSW, a clinician in private practice, presented the T4 story. They called the T4 helper cells the "quarterbacks" of the body's immune system, for it is these cells that call the shots around the body's ability to fight diseases. Unfortunately, the dreaded HIV virus enters the body in T4 cells. When this happens, some puzzling things occur. The virus just seems to lay dormant within these "quarterback" cells; very quiet, very adaptable to the environment.

Then, for some reason, the HIV virus "wakes up" and starts to replicate or reproduce itself, which it can easily do. The HIV virus continues to multiply until it finally breaks out and destroys the T4 helper cells, rendering the body's immune system defective. Once this happens the body is very vulnerable to a variety of unusual life-threatening illnesses.

It isn't the AIDS virus itself that kills, but because of the HIV-T4 cell activity, serious infections and cancers such as an infection of the lungs, Pneumocystis carinii penumonia (PCP), and a form of cancer called Kaposi's sarcoma (KS) can occur.

The HIV virus can damage a person's immune system, and when the immune system is out of commission, it can no longer keep you healthy. Once a person is HIV positive one of three things happen: (1) there are no symptoms at all; (2) AIDS-related complex (ARC) symptoms occur; or (3) A person gets AIDS.

ARC symptoms include night sweats, fever, weight loss, tiredness, swollen lymph nodes, oral thrush, and diarrhea. Needless to say, other diseases can cause these symptoms, too, so only your doctor can determine whether the symptoms are ARC or AIDS-related.

NOT CAUSED BY CASUAL CONTACT

Remember that the HIV infection is not caused by casual contact. You run the risk of the HIV virus entering your body by having sex that involves the sharing of bodily secretions, sharing "works" in intravenous drug use, or by receiving contaminated blood or blood products. This latter risk is rapidly being reduced by testing all blood donors for antibodies to the virus. As a matter of fact, the odds of contracting the HIV virus from a blood transfusion are now about one in 133,000 to 150,000, on a national level.

Babies can be victims if their infected mothers pass the virus on to them by breast milk or through the bloodstream during pregnancy or at the time of birth.

Let me repeat: There is *no* test for AIDS. What you are tested for is for antibodies against HIV. An antibody is really a protein that is made by your body in response to an infection. So if you *do* test reactive (positive) for the HIV antibody, this is what it means and what it *doesn't* mean:

Testing Positive

1. You have become infected with the virus that causes AIDS.

2. You are not only infected but you are *infectious*.
3. It does *not* mean you are definitely going to get AIDS. Currently 10–30 percent *will* develop AIDS within the first five years of becoming HIV infected.

Testing Negative

If you have been tested and the result is *nonreactive*—that is, negative—then it means that:

1. You do *not* have the virus.
2. You just got the virus and haven't yet had time to become positive on the test.
3. It *doesn't* mean that you are uninfected or immune.

You should be retested in six months to make sure that you are still negative, particularly if you have multiple sex partners. Above all, you must practice safer sex—and it doesn't matter if you are the active ("on top") or passive ("on the bottom") partner in anal or vaginal intercourse either. However being the passive or "bottom" partner is more risky.

THE IMPORTANCE OF CONDOMS

The kind of condom you use is very important. Condoms that are lubricated with nonoxynol-9 are the best, since spermicides that contain nonoxynol-9 can kill the HIV virus. You can further protect yourself by using condoms that have reservoir tips to collect the semen. It is also recommended to use latex condoms; theoretically, the HIV virus can pass through animal membrane condoms.

Use plenty of water-based lubrication on the outside of the rubber, and continue to apply more lubrication as needed, particularly since water-based lubricants dry out quickly.

Take your time. Most of the projects that I shared with you earlier in this book are not meant to rush sex anyhow, so taking the time for safer sex is important. You can help prevent your rubbers from breaking by taking the time to allow you and your partner to relax and not to rush things. It also makes for more gratifying orgasms.

One other note about the use of rubbers: Make certain to hold onto the condom when pulling out to keep it from slipping off the penis. Always check the expiration date on the condom package, and frankly, this is no place to spare a dime or two between using a really good, prelubricated with nonoxynol-9 rubber and a "bargain thriller" of some variety or other. Your life is at stake, and this is certainly no place to save a dollar or two.

SOME SAFER SEX TECHNIQUES

I've been urging you to keep practicing safer sex. However, you may be asking what that really means in relation to what is possible; what things can you do when you are practicing safer sex techniques? Well, here are some, but by no means all, of the ways that safer sex can be practiced.

You and your partner can share body to body rubbing, or "dry fucking."

You can engage in masturbation, either alone or with a partner. Massage is a wonderful way to be sexually aroused and satisfied while being perfectly safe. Hugging, dry kissing and petting, and using clean dildos and other sex toys that are *not shared* fall into the safer sex category.

You and your partner can engage in games of bondage with no exchange of blood, of course. You can watch videos, share fantasies while masturbating, or watch others or even show off (stripping) for others. You can ejaculate on unbroken skin. In other words almost anything can be practiced as safer sex if it does not involve the sharing of body fluids that may contain the virus.

UNSAFE SEX PRACTICES

Obviously, the most risky behaviors are anal and vaginal intercourse without a condom. Having a "blow job" (fellatio) without using a condom is risky, even if you pull out of the mouth before ejaculation.

Getting semen or urine in the mouth, anus, eyes, or open skin wounds is unsafe. You must not pierce skin or use needles or any other activity that involves the exchange of blood. Sharing dildos and other sex toys is not safe, nor is licking or using your tongue around your partner's anal area. Active or passive fisting is unsafe.

Mouth to mouth wet kissing could be unsafe, and so could having vaginal or anal intercourse even with a rubber if the rubber breaks. The same applies to having a blow job with a rubber if it breaks. What we are really saying here is that the only *sure* way not to contract the HIV virus is to not have sex. I don't think that's really a choice for most of you; surely for those of you that have been reading this book and trying to find new ways and techniques to replace the sex you had while drinking.

Just decreasing the numbers of your sexual partners isn't good enough anymore, since you are still at high risk to contract the HIV virus if you are having unsafe sex, particularly as the virus becomes more widespread. Scientists are working on a vaccine, but it appears to be years away.

If one of you has tested HIV positive and the other partner has tested HIV nonreactive or negative, you still must follow guidelines for safer sex *every* time you have sex, to prevent the spreading of the virus from the positive partner to the negative partner.

If both of you are HIV positive it means both of you have the virus. You should have safer sex even when with your infected partner to prevent reinfection or infection with other sexually transmitted diseases that may add to the risk of developing AIDS.

Hopefully, both you and your partner have tested nonreactive or negative for twelve months or more. Also, hopefully, neither of you has had sex with anyone else nor are you IV drug users, so you are probably not infected. If that is the case, then safer sex may not be necessary, but don't *assume*. If there is any doubt, retest and make sure.

BEING CHOOSEY ABOUT SEX PARTNERS

One way to prevent the spread of the virus, and also to ease your anxiety about becoming infected or about infecting others, is to choose sex partners who are HIV negative, assuming you are also negative. The same would apply if you are HIV reactive (positive). You are better off with another HIV positive partner, practicing safer sex, not reinfecting each other nor spreading the virus to others.

The decisions about your sex partners as well as your sex practices are, of course, strictly your own. What's important to remember about all that we've discussed here is that AIDS is a killer disease. It is a hidden enemy that can lie dormant within your body for years, not making its final assault on your before a life-saving vaccine is developed. No one knows for sure.

But the practice of safer sex, keeping yourself to only one sex partner, and hopefully never returning to the use of alcohol or IV drugs (*any* drug use for that matter), are the best lines of defense against this enemy.

Twelve

Sober Sex:
Beginning Again

My objective in writing this book has been to provide a set of guidelines that recovering people everywhere can follow to achieve a new dimension in their sexual lives. We have examined the importance of the relationship and the values of commitment, the joy of experimentation, the facing and conquering of fears of rejection and failure.

As I have been writing this book, the material has been stored in a file of my computer that I have named SOBERSEX. That file name led to its use as an acronym for what we have been exploring together in these pages, and it's really what I hope you will remember and use to learn, practice, experiment, and expand your sexual horizons without the old crutches of alcohol and drugs:

S • Satisfying
O • Open
B • Beautiful
E • Exciting
R • Rewarding

S • Sensual
E • Energized
X • Xtry (abbreviation for extraordinary)

Your sexual life has not ended with your sobriety; it is, in fact, just beginning, and beginning in a new and exciting fashion, with the emphasis on building your relationship.

It doesn't matter if you are not in a relationship at the moment; it doesn't matter if you are single, gay, lesbian, or in a relationship that has become stale and uninviting. There are certain basics that must be explored, signposts on your pathway to discovering and working a program of sex in sobriety.

COMMITMENT AS A GUIDE

I have emphasized your need for commitment—not only to your sexual partner but also to yourself—that you will try these new things, and that you will reengage your sexual life without returning to the use of drugs or alcohol.

Without commitment, there isn't much with which to build a relationship, or to experiment with any of the projects I have given you. It's much like an exercise program or a diet, isn't it? Without commitment to stick with the new plan and at least try with some sense of consistency and with a lot of individual effort, you will fail.

It is the same with sober sex. This is all new to you, and scary; the fear of rejection and the fear of failure hangs over you. Commitment is the helping hand that reinforces your pledge to make changes in your life, to try the new things and place the new planks of expectations and results in your relationship bridge.

No war or tennis match was ever won; no high school, college, or graduate education achieved; no picture painted; no book written; no music penned; no discovery made without a deep sense of commitment. Columbus continued what many thought was a crackpot journey that would lead him off the end of the earth, because he had a deep sense of commitment to the mission.

For you, a sense of having to make changes, of looking at new ways of doing things, of trying the projects, of opening the doors wider in your relationship, even failing, but failing honestly, in some of the new experiments of a sober sex life are all dependent upon your deep sense of commitment to make these changes.

I tell our patients over and over that give up the bottle or the pot or coke or whatever is just the *first* step in recovery. It is necessary to make changes in the way you do things and in the way you look at things, places, and people.

We have discovered that changes in the way you think about and perform sexual acts are also necessary. When you were drinking or drugging, things like commitment, communication, caring, sharing, and trust all lost importance. Frankly, the only thing that was important to you was sex itself—a selfish, noncommitted course of action that really lead nowhere in the long run.

BUILDING THE NEW BRIDGE

As you go back and read the chapters that deal with building that new bridge to your relationship, remember that I am not telling you how long or high your bridge has to be. You are the architect of that bridge; how it will serve you and your partner is up to you. The strength of your design will be measured by the success of your sexual engagements. If you don't want to expend the effort that is required to put those new planks in place, then you may as well forget this book and treat sober sex as too much work for you.

So many patients over the years have told me how they have been disappointed by their sex life after they regained sobriety that I knew there was a need for ways to explore how sexuality and sensuality change when one gains sobriety. I knew there was a need to show how sex in sobriety could be fulfilling.

I'm asking you to free your mind, to open up the vistas of sober sex. That means applying the energy that one wastes wondering whether you should be a couple into actually *being* a couple, doing couple kinds of things and generally building those relationship planks.

WILLINGNESS TO TRY

To make this book work for you requires that you make this pledge: "I will try these things not just once but two or three times. I will make a sincere effort to explore these ideas fully and discard what doesn't work for me, but keep, expand, and practice the things that do work."

That's really all that's required. You need to be willing to look at how things can be different from what they had been before. If you are successful in ridding your mental closet of everything that didn't work for you sexually, and look at what might work as I have outlined it, then you are on your way to enjoying the sex and sobriety that I know is available.

I mentioned that I was interested in hearing from you about the techniques, ideas, and exercises that are in this book. Take a moment and write to me, won't you? There is nothing quite so gratifying to me as reading letters and cards from people who have felt compelled to correspond with me after reading my book.

If there are things you like, if there are things you take exception to, or just want to comment, get to that typewriter or word processor, or pad, pen or pencil and write:

Jack Mumey
Gateway Treatment Center
1191 South Parker Road, Suite 100
Denver, CO 80231

I hope that you are motivated to try the things in this book, for they will make a difference in your life if you let them. You have to be willing to discard the old ways the same way you have discarded a life of drinking alcohol and using drugs.

There is a great reward to rediscovering your sexual and sensual self in a life free from alcohol and in a state of sobriety. There is an even greater reward to making a commitment to change, to exploration along the paths of reawakening of the sexual being you can be, sharing the love and beauty and joy of your life with a special someone.

Your sexual self has been asleep, befuddled and fogged with alcohol or some other drug. But now you can awaken those fires that have only been smoldering. You can decide that one of the rewards for your sobriety and being clean from drugs is to really find your sexual self.

This can and will be a new you. A person who is beginning to be comfortable with him/herself, with who you are and with whom you have cast your life. It's more exciting than you can imagine and you only have to unlock the doors of your imagination to continue building on the foundation I have started for you.

YOU ARE THE BUILDER

If I have been the architect, then surely you are the master builder, and how the project starts and finishes rests with the efforts you and your partner, whether straight, gay, or lesbian, are willing to make.

If you are a single person, then the manner in which you rediscover your sexual being, and the steps you are willing to take to enter again the exotic and fulfilling world of your own sexuality, depends on the effort you are willing to expend.

Each and every person who has started down the road of personal recovery has faced unknown fears, has perhaps even considered returning to alcohol and drugs because the fear of sexual failures and rejections were too much without their addictive crutches.

So many people have shared that thought with me that I

know it is not an isolated idea. To these people I again say, "trust the process" of sex in sobriety. Follow the plans, the outlines, the relationship building, the goal setting, the projects and the new mind-set that I have outlined for you.

THE PRIORITY OF CONTINUED SOBRIETY

Above all, keeping your sobriety and your state of drug-free living must be a priority. If you relapse, if you return to alcohol and drugs because of the fears of a lost, diminished, or unexciting and unrewarding, dismal, sex life, then you will have failed miserably to understand what this book is all about.

What is written on these pages works; I implore you to put your energies into trying my ideas. This is *not* the end; it is the beginning of a new and outward-bound journey for you in the realm of the sexuality that every man and woman so richly deserves.

This is a chance to begin fresh, new, exciting, and rewarding adventures in a sensual and sexual world that you once blocked out with alcohol and drugs. How thrilling for you to rediscover who you are and what you have to give to a relationship, or just yourself in a state of awareness, clarity, commitment, and *sharing* the wonders of your mind and your body as they have emerged from the darkness of the addiction to which you were a slave.

In the words of William Wordsworth, the fire of your sober sexuality waits for you to stir and take action.

O joy! that in our embers
Is something that doth live.
That nature yet remembers
What was so fugitive!

Bibliography

BOOKS

Barbach, Lonnie Garfield. *For Yourself: The Fulfillment of Female Sexuality*. New York: Signet, 1976.

Braun, Walter. *Intercourse Illustrated*. Palm Springs, Calif.: Merchandise for Mailers, 1981.

Comfort, Alex, ed. *The Joy of Sex, A Gourmet Guide to Love Making*. New York: Simon & Schuster, 1972.

――― . *More Joy, A Lovemaking Companion to The Joy of Sex*. New York: Crown Publishers, 1974.

De Angeles, Barbara. *How to Make Love All the Time, Secrets for Making Love Work*. New York: Rawson Associates, 1987.

Fisher, Seymour. *The Female Orgasm*. New York: Basic Books, 1973.

Forrest, Gary G. *Alcoholism and Human Sexuality*. Springfield, Ill.: Charles C. Thomas, 1983.

Friday, Nancy. *Men in Love, Men's Sexual Fantasies: The Triumph of Love Over Rage*. New York: Dell Publishing, 1981.

――― . *My Mother/My Self, The Daughter's Search for Identity*. New York: Dell Publishing, 1977.

———— · *My Secret Garden. Women's Sexual Fantasies.* New York: Pocket Books, 1973.

Heiman, Julia; Leslie LoPiccolo; and Joseph LoPiccolo. *Becoming Orgasmic: A Sexual Growth Program for Women.* Englewood Cliffs, N.J.: Prentice-Hall, 1976.

Inkeles, Gordon, and Murray Todris. *The Art of Sensual Massage.* New York: Simon & Schuster, 1972.

Kaplan, H. S. *Disorders Of Sexual Desire.* New York: Brunner/Mazel, 1979.

Kassorla, Irene K. *Nice Girls Do.* New York: Berkley Books, 1984.

Katchadourian, Herant A., and Donald T. Lunde. *Fundamentals of Human Sexuality.* New York: Holt, Rinehart and Winston, 1972.

Kinsey, A. C.; W. B. Pomeroy; and C. E. Martin. *Sexual Behavior in the Human Male.* Philadelphia: W. B. Saunders, 1948.

Kinsey, A. C.; W. B. Pomeroy; C. E. Martin; and P. H. Gebhard. *Sexual Behavior in the Human Female.* New York: Pocket Books, 1965.

Lang, Alan R., and Deborah I. Frank. "Chronic Alcohol Use and Sexual Dysfunction." *Journal of Clinical Practice in Sexuality,* Vol. 5, No. 8.

Masters, W. H., and V. E. Johnson. *Human Sexual Inadequacy.* Boston: Little, Brown, 1970.

Nellis, Muriel. *The Female Fix.* Boston: Houghton Mifflin, 1980.

Nin, Anais. *Delta of Venus.* New York: Harcourt Brace Jovanovich, 1969.

O'Connor, Sean. *The Photographic Guide to Sexual Secrets.* Chatsworth, Calif.: Media Press, 1987.

Yorke, Andrew. *The Art of Erotic Massage.* London: Javelin Books, 1988.

Ziskin, Jay, and Mae Ziskin. *The Extra-Marital Sex Contract.* Los Angeles: Nash Publishing, 1973.

VIDEO CASSETTES

Love Skills, a Guide to the Pleasures of Sex, MCA-TV 1984.

Playboy's Secrets of Euromassage, HBO Home Video.

Playboy's Sensual Secrets of Oriental Massage, HBO Home Video.

Index